VIETNAM
BEYOND

By Gerald E. Augustine

UNITED STATES ARMY
October 5, 1965- August 4, 1967

196th LIGHT INFANTRY BRIGADE
3rd Battalion / 21st Infantry - 2nd Platoon
October 5, 1965 – March 5, 1967
Machine Gun Squad

4th INFANTRY DIVISION
2nd Battalion / 12th Infantry – 3rd Platoon
March 5, 1967 – August 4, 1967
Rifle Squad

DORRANCE
PUBLISHING CO
EST. 1920
PITTSBURGH, PENNSYLVANIA 15238

Dorrance Publishing Co
585 Alpha Drive
Pittsburgh, PA 15238
Visit our website at *www.dorrancebookstore.com*

ISBN: 978-1-6386-7193-0
eISBN: 978-1-6386-7722-2

VIETNAM
BEYOND

By Gerald E. Augustine

UNITED STATES ARMY
October 5, 1965- August 4, 1967

196th LIGHT INFANTRY BRIGADE
3rd Battalion / 21st Infantry - 2nd Platoon
October 5, 1965 – March 5, 1967
Machine Gun Squad

4th INFANTRY DIVISION
2nd Battalion / 12th Infantry – 3rd Platoon
March 5, 1967 – August 4, 1967
Rifle Squad

PROLOGUE

WE ARE VIETNAM VETERANS. When our country called, we responded by either joining the military or answering the draft. The day we were inducted, whether it be the Army, Navy, Marines, Air Force, or the Coast Guard, we had no idea where we were headed. The important thing is we served honorably.

When we returned home from that unpopular war, we weren't greeted with accolades, parades, or for that matter, much respect. We had to blend back into civilian life ourselves. It wasn't easy. Now that many years have passed since we returned, a half century, we are finally getting some respect and recognition that we so well-deserve. Our mission will remain the same. We will educate middle and high school students and teach them the history of our war and that joining the military is an honorable path to take for their future if they so choose. We will also abide by the term "Veterans Helping Veterans." Whenever there is a veteran in need, we shall come to his or her aid and help them appropriately.

I am truly honored to be amongst you. You can be proud that you are a Vietnam Veteran and served our great country, the United States of America.

Gerald E. Augustine

DEDICATION

I would like to dedicate my book to all the recipients of the Combat Infantry-man's Badge, (C.I.B.). It is awarded to infantrymen in the rank of colonel and below who fought in active ground combat while assigned as members of either an infantry or special forces unit of brigade size or smaller at any time after December 6th, 1941. It is awarded also to warrant officers with an infantry or special forces MOS.

It was created during WWII to highlight the achievements of those tasked to fight in combat zones on the front lines. It was recognized that the infan-tryman continuously operated under the worst conditions and performed mis-sions that was not assigned to other soldiers or units. The infantry, a small portion of the total armed forces, was suffering the most casualties while re-ceiving the least public recognition. The wars have demonstrated the impor-tance of highly proficient, tough, hard, and aggressive infantry, which can be obtained by developing a high degree of individual all-around proficiency on the part of every infantryman. That is why the C.I.B. was established for in-fantry personnel. The C.I.B. badge is the highest award officially authorized with an executive order dated November 15th, 1943. The eligibility require-ments 1. Be an infantryman satisfactorily performing infantry duties. 2. As-signed to an infantry unit during such time as the unit is engaged in active ground combat. 3. Actively participate in such ground combat. Campaign or battle credit alone is not sufficient for the award of the C.I.B. The recipient must be personally present and under hostile fire while serving in an assigned infantry of special forces primary duty to close with and destroying the enemy with direct fires. It is somewhat of common knowledge that the worst job on earth is that of being a combat infantryman. It was also common knowledge to the combat infantryman in Vietnam that there were seven soldiers confined to the rear in duty, such as construction, maintenance, administration, and protection of base facilities to every one-soldier serving in the front lines. 86 percent of those serving in Vietnam were in the rear. To the combat infantryman, those soldiers were referred to as REMF's, (Rear Echelon M-F's) or PUKES. That is why I wish to dedicate my book to those who have earned the Combat Infantryman's Badge.

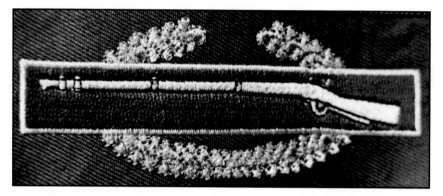

CIB

INTRODUCTION

Thinking back to fifty-seven years ago when I was drafted into the Army at nineteen years of age, I was enjoying the best of times. It was during the summer of '65 when I was on a break from attending the University of Connecticut. I was knee deep into my hobby of building my own "Hot-Rod" and attending the weekly drag races at Connecticut Drag-way in Colchester, only twenty miles from my home in Middletown, Connecticut. I was also working along with my dad at his self- employed roofing business. I was abruptly being pulled away from the best years of my life. I didn't question my being drafted as I believed that it was my duty to serve my country. So October 5th, 1965 was the day that I was to board the bus at the Middletown post office and head to New Haven, Connecticut and on to Fort Dix, New Jersey for my induction into the United States Army's 196th Light Infantry Brigade.

I had twelve weeks of summer fun to prepare myself to be away from "the world" for two years. I continued to work as a roofer's helper earning as much money as I could, which went into my '40 Ford street machine to make it aesthetically better and faster. I raced it on July 24th at Connecticut Dragway, winning a "B" Gas trophy. I had recently installed a 425 H.P. "409" engine that I purchased from my future brother in-law. I partied with my friends, attended the "drags," and worked with my dad right up to leaving for "who knows where" and wondering if I would ever return to the "good life."

I am writing this book to let the readers know what a Vietnam combat veteran had to endure and what the future had in store for him. I realize that every veteran has his own story to tell. I feel that mine is quite unique. I hope you enjoy it.

HELP THOSE WHO REMEMBER

VIETNAM

TEACH THOSE WHO DON'T

Chapters

1. My Roots

A Native of Middletown, My Dad

As I was growing up on Ridge Road in Middletown, Connecticut, I was always eager to listen to my dad tell his stories of growing up in the south end of this lovely town where I still call home. He was born in 1910 and was raised in the area then known as "Duck Hollow." It was a predominately Polish neighborhood where East Main Street crosses Union Street and south and east of that location. It does not exist today, as Personal Auto Care, Connecticut Rental, and the YMCA parking lot occupy some of that space today. At eleven years of age, my father, Edward Augustine, became an orphan. His parents passed on due to one of the many diseases that were prevalent at the time. From then on, various Polish families would take my dad in, so he would have a family to call his own. He attended St. Mary School on South Main Street until the eighth grade when he found that he needed to make a living at that time of his life. There were many factories and mills in Middletown then, and my dad worked in many of them. Some mentioned to me were The Goodyear Rubber Co., Wilcox Lace Shop, Russell Manufacturing, and he even helped build the Middletown-Portland bridge. He boxed at Coleman's carnival and was the high diver of Middletown. On Sunday afternoons, in the hot summer months, cars would line up along the river, right about where Harbor Park is now, to watch his dive. My dad's friend at the time, Nate Gilletti, would collect change and rarely some paper money from the spectators. My dad had a skeleton key that allowed him to access the control tower of a coal chute derrick, so he could walk out to the end to accomplish his dive. My dad told me this activity went on weekly until one day, he caught his friend Nate with a five-dollar bill rolled up and stuck in his ear. I believe that ended a long friendship and a popular summer family attraction. In later years, Mr. Gilletti owned and operated Gilletti's Service Station, which was located on Main Street Extension, where the CVS Pharmacy is now located. In the 1950's, I hung around that station because there was also a Dairy Queen adjacent to the property. It was only a half-mile from my home. At that time, Mr. Gilletti had had a tracheotomy and had to speak with a chrome speaking devise up against his throat, which had a small open hole. If he didn't use the device, you could barely hear him. He had the derogatory nickname labeled on him as, "The Whispering Bandit." I believe that was derived from the ordeal with my dad's diving and Mr. Gilletti collecting the donations. My dad joined the army in 1936 or 1937 and served in the Hawaiian Islands. I think Ford Field was mentioned when he discussed his time in the army. When he was discharged and returned home to Middletown, he was hired to work on the new Middletown-Portland bridge that was being constructed. He talked about going under water in the diving-bell chambers, and that you couldn't stay under for too long or you would "get-the-bends," a slang term for a crippling condition. He also mentioned work on top of the arches having no protection whatsoever. At one time, he was painting the top of the arches when he had to urinate badly. Instead of climbing all the way down, he just went in the paint and stirred it up. If you think about it, this must have happened often. One day his foreman got angry at him for wearing leather soled shoes while walking on top of the arches. Of course he had to change into soft soled boots from then on. I have a great photo of my dad as he worked on the bridge. It is in the commemorative booklet that was issued on August 6th, 1938, the grand opening and ceremony of the first bridge crossing. Around this time, my dad met my mom, Elizabeth Sebranski, who moved to Middletown from Troy, New York. She grew up in Troy and lost her mother when she was eleven-years-old. My grandfather, William, had a tough time bringing up and supporting six daughters and a son while working at a factory to make ends meet. My mom, therefore, moved to Middletown to live with her aunt, Mrs. Warrenda, to take some of the burden off her dad. My mom and dad met and were soon married in 1939. They told me they had a five-dollar model "A" Ford and drove to Baltimore, Maryland to get "hitched." My dad was twenty-eight-years-old, and my mom, a mature fourteen. Their first apartment was called "Hoberman's," which is still situated on South Main

Street, a few doors from St. Mary School. Being dirt-poor during their early years together, they found numerous ways to earn a "buck." One method was selling Christmas trees on Main Street. My dad learned this trade by working at Millane's Nurseries in Cromwell, Connecticut. Working at Millane's was not a pleasant experience for my dad and his friends. As it was told to me by my dad, he and his buddies would be driven in Millane's old antique trucks, in the beginning of December, to New Hampshire to cut and collect hundreds of Christmas trees. The trucks were all 1930's vintage, having no heat in them what-so-ever. My dad talked about how freezing cold it was as if it were yesterday. He never forgot it. After those harrowing experiences, my dad found a way to get heated trucks, along with his friends, and went to get his own trees to sell. It became quite lucrative at the time. I think back to these "good-old" days that my dad told me about and realize that my dad became somewhat of an entrepreneur under his own accord. In the summer of 1941, my dad was working at the Russell Manufacturing Corporation. This is where asbestos clutch, belting, and brake linings were produced. Stop & Shop supermarket, on East Main Street occupies the land now. It was during World War II, parachute webbing, shoulder-harnesses, and other types of web gear was also contracted for the U.S. government war effort. One hot afternoon while working at the "Russell," the sky literally opened up to a torrential downpour. The roof began to leak over machinery, so my dad's foreman asked him to go up on the roof to see what he could do to stop the water from coming in. My dad was very handy, his foreman knew this, as he had worked at various factories and venues throughout town so he was trusted to take on just about any task at hand. My dad needed some roofing tar to patch the leaks, so was confided to go purchase a five-gallon pail of roof cement at the local hardware store. As he was purchasing the needed material, he asked the clerk for a discount.

The clerk responded with, "What is your company name?"

My dad, in a subdued manner, glanced down at the pail of roof cement and read the label, "No Leak Roof Cement."

So my dad replied to the clerk, "No leak roofing company." My dad received his discount and returned to the "sweat-shop," as he called it, and told his friends and co-workers that he was going into the roofing business. He left the "Russell," purchased some tools and an old beat-up truck, and was on his way. He worked mostly on shingling and repairs until an employee of his, John Kulmatz, suggested for him to buy a "hot-tar kettle." My dad did just that, and his business took off and became quite successful. While my dad was running his business in the late forties, sometimes he would leave work early to pick my mom up at her job at Wilcox Lace Corporation, which was located at the corner of Cooley Avenue and Main Street Extension. I was brought along a few times to see the work in action. I remember all the women lined up working in front of huge machines. The noise was astounding. It was when I heard, for the first time, new terms spoken, "piece work," "winding bobbins," "bolts-of lace," etcetera. I got to take some cardboard cones home for souvenirs. They were used to wind pure silk threads on them. There were thousands of them in use above the ladies at their work stations. It was fascinating at my age to watch the whole production. Piece work was when the employed put out as much product as they were able, and so desired, and would get paid accordingly. I heard, at the time, that my mother was very good at her job and was one of the best producers. She and my dad worked together to live the American dream. They were able to purchase their first home in 1951. It was on Ridge Road, a charming section of town. My dad was working for a council member at the town hall, and the house was offered to him for $5,000. It was quite run-down, but we were able to refurbish it in due time. It included a double lot where we would raise many animals and have great vegetable gardens. I remember during the fifties my dad bringing home the lunch counter stool seats from various diners, restaurants, and coffee shops. Through the night, our family became an assembly line in our kitchen. We re-upholstered hundreds of seats and had them ready for early the following morning when my dad returned them to the establishments. I recall he received $3 apiece, great money at the time, as my parent's mortgage was only $21 a month. To top it off, the material used was discarded remnants from an upholstery factory in town that my dad collected for free at the town dump. 1951 was also the year our family was hit with some devastating news. My dad was overcome with tuberculosis. Our family was quarantined while my dad spent one full year in Newington and Uncasville, Connecticut sanitariums. He was admitted during Thanksgiving week 1951 and released Thanksgiving week 1952. He had two major operations that lasted seven and eight hours respectively that resulted in the removal of his right lung. He was advised to never go back to the strenuous roofing work and to never smoke again. During this time, my mother took driving lessons and got a job in Deep River, Connecticut at a garment factory. She had been my dad's secretary for the family roofing business, which was now out of business. Sad to say, when my dad returned home from the hospital, he took up smoking again that lasted the rest of his life. The good news is he returned to his roofing vocation and was fortunate to work until he retired at age sixty-five. I remember the weekends while in high school and the summer months operating the hot-tar-kettle and learning the trade. I still have it in my barn and could fire it up anytime. There are many, many roofing stories that go along with that kettle. Chapters could be written about it. My dad passed on in 1983 of complications of leukemia. My mom passed on in 2000 of complications of emphysema. God bless my wonderful parents.

DAD AND AUTHOR

DAD WORKING ON MIDDLETOWN-PORTLAND BRIDGE
PHOTO FROM GRAND OPENING BROCHURE AUGUST 6TH, 1938

DAD (ON LEFT) ARMY IN HAWAII

Dad and Mom (Ed and Betty)

Dad on rt. with hot-tar kettle for built-up roofing

My son Marc with Dad's old sign

2. Where am I From

When asked where I am from, I have no reason to think of an answer. I have lived in Middletown, Connecticut for seventy-six years, except for the twenty-two months that I was away serving my country in the military. I currently live on Ridge Road. I have lived on Ridge Road in three different houses since 1950. I have never lived more than one mile from where I was born at Middlesex Hospital. My grammar school is just one quarter mile south from my present home, and my junior and senior high school is just a quarter mile west of my home. On my current property is the former neighborhood grocery store where I used to buy my candies and goodies on the way to and from school. My eldest son lives in my old homestead a quarter mile north on Ridge Road. There is no reason for any changes in my living arrangements at this time. I am very comfortable at my location in my town, and I truly enjoy living in a town with so much history and heritage.

Middletown is centrally located in Connecticut at the "bend in the river," the Connecticut River that is. It was a leading seaport and industrial site since being founded in 1650. It was suggested to be the capital of Connecticut before Hartford was eventually chosen. It is a university city where Wesleyan University was established in 1831. It has one of the widest main streets in the nation. Recently it has become a leading restaurant destination for the dining folk.

Growing up in Middletown was always adventurous. Main street was only a half mile from my home where three movie theaters prospered, The Capital, the Palace, and the Middlesex. The Middlesex was a former vaudeville theater back in the teens and twenties. It was always a treat to attend the "Middlesex," as it was the fanciest theater in town. It seemed that it was only opened for special films that would be shown and would draw a larger crowd than usual. Other great activities that we could be a part of and enjoy that were right in town were roller skating, ten pin bowling, duck pin bowling, swimming at many lakes and ponds, and boating right on the river. There was also skiing at Powder Ridge, the home of the infamous Powder Ridge Rock Festival of 1969.

Another famous establishment founded in Middletown over a hundred years ago is Colemans' Carnival, which tours the country annually to this day. Every year in April, it begins its tour right on the same street where it all began.

Middletown was also the center of the manufacturing of weapons before and during the civil war where the Simeon North and the Starr families and others provided muskets, pistols, swords, etcetera for the U.S. Army, civilians, and others.

Other well-known companies that called Middletown its home was The Goodyear Rubber Co., Remington-Rand Typewriter, Russell Manufacturing Co., Wilcox-Crittenden Marine Hardware, Kane Brick Co., Wilcox Lace Co., and Pratt & Whitney Aircraft, formerly called CANEL (Connecticut Advanced Nuclear Engine Lab). It is also a fact that the Indian Motorcycle Co. was founded at the turn of the 20th century by two gentlemen in a garage near Traverse Square.

The best-known fact, I feel, is that Middletown honors its veterans to the highest degree. The most beautiful monuments are displayed in a row on a state route which runs through the center of town. The Connecticut State Veterans Cemetery is also located in Middletown.

There are many, many more interesting facts about my home town that could fill volumes. I am proud to be a native of Middletown, Connecticut. There is no reason to leave my roots.

CONNECTICUT CIVIL WAR

BLUE AND GOLD STAR MEMORIALS

GULF WAR OF 1990 TO PRESENT CONFLICTS

WW II

WW I

KOREA-VIETNAM

A NATIONAL MONUMENT —DESIGNED AND DONATED BY DAV CHAPTER #7

Both photos of Veterans Park, Middletown, CT

3. Becoming A Soldier

I was nineteen-years-old at the time in the summer of 1965, not really knowing where the rest of my life was headed. I received my draft notice and was a little overwhelmed. I was a student on summer break from the University of Connecticut, Hartford branch. The classrooms were so over crowded that there was standing room only. This was due to the Vietnam conflict going on. I didn't question the notice, as I felt it was my duty to serve. I had about two and a half months before I had to board the bus on October 5th to head to New Haven, then onto Fort Dix, New Jersey to begin basic training, or so I thought. The Army had other ideas for me. So during this waiting period, I still enjoyed my car hobby, working along with my dad and hanging out with my buddies at night. I also had a steady girlfriend that would go along with me most of the time. I was also keeping up with my weight training in the basement of my house. While I was a senior in high school, a friend of mine, John Mazzotta, brought me to the Hartford Barbell Studio, located just off of the beginning of Main Street in downtown Hartford, Connecticut. While visiting there for the first time, I was so impressed with the builds and the strengths of the guys training there. Little did I know at the time that weight training would become another passion of mine and would have a life-long effect on my legacy. That year I requested a weight set for Christmas and was pleased that I received one. I was still frequenting Hartford Barbell Studio, mostly on weekends, with my friend John to get a good work-out in.

October 5th came too soon. As our bus load from Middlesex County disembarked to Fort Dix, the occupants suddenly realized when looking around that this certainly was going to be a new life style. We were now recruits in the U. S. Army. During the two weeks' time we spent at Fort Dix, waiting for our next assignment, our heads were shaved, medical and intelligence tests were performed. We were told that other recruits would be arriving from the Midwest, upper New York state, and from New Jersey, Virginia, and southern east coast regions. During my time at Fort Dix, I began to notice that recruits of a smaller stature or of being weak or nimble would often be harassed or picked on more often than not. I made up my mind that this wasn't going to happen to me. I made it a point to continue with my strength training, it being with weights, free hand, or make do with what was available at the time. We were housed in old wooden barracks that had old metal bunk beds. Each night I would push the bunk beds close together until they were a shoulders width apart. I would then proceed to do sets of twenty-five shoulder dips between them. I was also performing sets of push-ups on my own during the night time lulls. When the other recruits finally arrived, it didn't take long for us to muster together and find out that we were headed to Ayer, Massachusetts, home of Fort Devens, to begin basic training with the newly reactivated 196th Light Infantry Brigade. During all of our training, we were never told that the 196th was a unit to be deployed to Vietnam. We were constantly told that we were headed to South America for "police action."

We then traveled to Fort Devens by a caravan of buses. When we disembarked, we were greeted by columns of seasoned soldiers. I must say, the site was pretty impressive. Here was a bunch of raggedy-ass teenagers only interested in their car and/or girlfriend that they left behind and were not interested in becoming a spit shined trooper. This would end quite abruptly as the drill instructors immediately took over the situation. I then found out that I would be part of the 3rd battalion, 21st Infantry. We looked around at our new home away from home and were a little taken aback. Our barracks consisted of new three-story brick billets. We thought that we were a privileged bunch. Little did we know we probably just lucked out. Our billets were modern compared to the other battalions that had to reside in the old WWII wooden barracks. We even had shiny tiled floors, modern bathrooms, and recreation rooms with color TVs. Believe me, the rec-rooms saw little use during basic training.

THE '40 FORD I LEFT BEHIND THAT I BUILT IN MY BACK YARD.

THE 196TH LIGHT INFANTRY BRIGADE — "THE CHARGERS"

4. Training and More Training

Looking back at my time in basic training, it seemed very odd that we trained right through the dead of winter surviving the tundra of the New England blizzards, freezing cold, and deep snow. Why was this when we were told we were to be deployed to the tropics in South America.

During basic training at Fort Devens, I lifted weights every chance I could. This wasn't much because every minute of every day was accounted for. When we weren't out in the field, we were in classrooms. When we weren't in the classrooms or in the fields, we were either on K.P. or we were out on guard duty. When we were in our rooms, we were supposed to be studying or taking care of our gear and uniforms. The results of keeping up my strength did pay off however. At the hand grenade training day, I was able to throw the hand grenade far beyond the limit of the range. One of the platoon leaders, Lt. Lawson, stated that I would be throwing the javelin in the upcoming battalion track meet. That surprised me because I was never on any sports team in high school. When the day came, I was pretty fortunate to win the javelin throw in the battalion meet with no form whatsoever. That accomplishment put me into the forthcoming post meet. I was able to borrow some other recruits track shoes during the post meet. They helped immensely. I wished I would have trained with them before the meets. The three winning throws happened to land in a three-foot triangle. My throw was awarded third place overall. Previously I had never thrown the javelin, so this achievement sparked an inner desire to excel in other ventures.

After basic training, a short break and some three day passes, the entire brigade headed Northwest to Camp Drum near Watertown, New York, near the Canadian border. It was in April of 1966 where we would be training in A.I.T. or Advanced Infantry Training. At Fort Devens, spring had sprung, and the weather was to everyone's liking. We were totally fed up with the training in the freezing cold. Our high hopes of training in the much-improved weather of spring changed drastically when we arrived at Camp Drum. It was like going back into the dead of winter. Most of the training ended up being in the deep snow and in frigid temperatures, just like it was at Fort Devens. We couldn't win.

New Fatigues

The daily training regime was different from basic training. It was almost like a normal job. After morning P.T. (physical training) and a good hearty breakfast, we would either patrol out to the ranges or hop on a deuce and a half, (2-1/2-ton military transport truck) and ride out quite far to no-man's land. There we would practice general combat soldiering and set up defensive positions. In most cases, we would head back to our barracks before dark. We would have dinner, then the time was ours to do what we wanted. Most guys went to the dining hall that doubled as a recreation room. There was a large gymnasium complex not too far from our barracks. I would walk there each night with a couple of buddies to lift weights. Being twenty-years-old I was impressionable and believed what I read and most of what I was told. I happened to buy a fitness magazine and read an article on how to "bulk-up" and gain strength in a short period of time. I followed the course diligently. I had been very interested in fitness right from the beginning of my induction. Whenever there was a time out from training, being in classrooms, marching, or in the field to break the monotony, the guys would relieve themselves by picking on one another. It was a fun thing to do and was called "grab-ass." Of course the men of smaller or weaker stature would be picked on the most. When all the guys were wrestling or running around seeking another opponent, some would run toward me haphazardly and then think twice and veer off in another direction. I would chuckle to myself, but it instilled in me to keep the weight training up.

Back to the magazine that I purchased. The article stated that one could gain ten pounds of muscle and the strength would come along with it. You would do heavy squats with as much weight as you could handle. The same with bench presses and heavy arm curls with a straight bar. At night you would drink large volumes of milk, actually force drink it all through the night. The transformation to me was incredible. After dinner I would take six to eight cartons of milk from the mess hall and sip it through the night. I kept them on the window sill while the window pain was opened about eight inches. I went from 190 pounds to 214 pounds while at Camp Drum. One night I walked into the dining hall after my nightly training session. It seemed like everyone turned in my direction and laughed. My fatigues were shrinking so it seemed. My sleeves were halfway up my arms. My shirt buttons were ready to pop. My trousers were skin tight. Headquarters company wasn't too thrilled about issuing me a whole new wardrobe, which they did. One night when entering the dining hall, where most guys were playing cards, b-s-ing, or drinking beer, a bunch of northern New York farm boys challenged me to arm wrestling. Stanley Buyea was the champ from his parts. Wouldn't you know it, I cleaned house and was titled the arm-wrestling champ of our company. It brought a lot of respect along with it.

Missing Squad

During the advanced infantry training at Camp Drum, there was a lot of company, platoon, and squad-sized training plans. One of these consisted of our battalion heading out for five days into the wasteland, which was covered with about two feet of snow. It was so freezing cold and uncomfortable that we all hated it. We were to practice general combat soldiering and set up defensive positions. This was to be our jungle and gorilla war training. We were to learn about ambushes, booby traps, and proper defensive tactics at our NDP (night defensive positions). Well, we didn't like it. How could we do jungle training in deep snow while being so cold? We got right down to business and were sent out to the wilderness into the frozen tundra. We couldn't get over all the porcupines occupying the surrounding treetops. Also, the beaver dams were in abundance in all the streams and ponds we passed along the way. These were sights of Mother Nature at her best. Eventually we were ordered to patrol out in squad-sized groups and set up for the night. Our squad leader was of the mischievous and daring type and had a plan. We found a huge pine tree that had its lower branches hugging the ground. We proceeded to prop up the branches and dig our foxhole. We found that the more we dug, the warmer the hole became. We also noticed that our position was pretty much secluded from everyone else. By the time dusk arrived, we had a room underground that housed our squad of about eight men. The dirt was hidden under the snow. We camouflaged the surroundings, and our entrance was under the pine boughs. We had plenty of candles, flashlights, C-rations, and Sterno to keep the coffee hot. There were also playing cards to pass the time, so we wouldn't get bored. I think back now how funny it was when an alert was put out for the missing squad that couldn't be found. We got lost in the shuffle because of the size of the operation. All we got was a good tongue lashing, especially the squad leader, when we emerged from our bunker when the mission was over. All the other trainees envied us at what we accomplished.

FAMILY TIME

While we were finishing up our time at Camp Drum, three-day passes were handed out for the following weekend. Every time we had the chance, we wanted to spend some time with our families and friends at home. Home sickness never went away. We were released late Friday afternoon and we were to return by curfew at midnight Sunday evening. Many crowded into cars, so they split the costs of heading to their home states of New Jersey, Ohio, Michigan, and Connecticut, just to name a few of the destinations. I had the opportunity to borrow a black 1961 Chevy Corvair from my friend Jack who was on duty for the weekend. Three of my close friends who were from towns close to mine piled into the car with me. We couldn't get away fast enough. We made it as far as Albany, and the rear end of the Corvair froze up. The four of us got out and pushed the car to the nearest gas station. It just so happened it was also a service center. I spoke to the attendant, and he said that he could repair the car and it would be ready in about a week to ten days. I then called Jack back at Camp Drum and he said that he would call the station and give them the okay to go ahead with the work. Money was so scarce, we didn't know how Jack was going to pay for it. Army pay for a private was about $70 a month at the time. So there we were, stuck in Albany, New York on a Friday night. My three buddies looked at me for a solution to make it home. My mother just so happened to be from Troy, the next town over, so I gave her a call in

Middletown and told her our predicament. She immediately drove the 130 miles and picked us up and drove us back to Middletown. God bless my mom. The two days spent at home went by so quickly. One of the friends that came along with me was able to borrow a car, so we could return on time to the base on Sunday night. We made it right on time. Two weeks later, Jack was issued a three-day pass for the weekend and went home with another friend. He was returning to Camp Drum on Sunday afternoon when he stopped in Albany to pick up his Corvair, which was repaired and parked outside the station which happened to be closed. Lucky for Jack, he had a spare key with him. Unlucky for the station owner, he never got paid for the rear end repairs. He was probably frightened at what to tell the owner when he called that his car was stolen from his lot. Jack sure was happy to get his car back.

MORE TRAINING

When we headed back to Fort Devens, we found out that spring finally had arrived. We were so happy that the snow was gone and it was warmer. The army had another surprise for us. The entire brigade was headed to Camp Edwards Air Force Base on Cape Cod for two weeks. There we would be a part of A.U.T. or advanced unit training. That would be the fine tuning of all the battalions and support groups. It comes to mind how gullible we were. All this training was for police action in some country in South America? The training was fairly general at Camp Edwards. More routine soldiering. By now we felt that we had had enough. After the two weeks, we headed back to Fort Devens for more of routine soldiering. I guess the Army felt too much training is still not enough.

AN ARMY TRADITION

While back at Fort Devens, our complete brigade was called to formation on the parade grounds one evening. The announcement was made that we were to be deployed to Vietnam. A solemness came over everyone. A couple of mornings later, word got around that a soldier had hung himself in one of the abandoned barracks. Everyone felt remorse. Within the next few days, it was announced that there would be a battalion-sized guard duty formation. On that day, there were over 400 men to be inspected. A challenge was made that if a soldier earned the position of Colonel's orderly, he would fly to Vietnam with the advanced party, a three-day trip. The brigade would sail to Vietnam from Boston, on through the Panama Canal, then to California and onto Vietnam, a thirty-three day voyage. The transport ships would be the Alexander Patch and the Darby. No one wanted to sail on either of these two scows. The heat and humidity would become unbearable. With the hundreds of troops on board, approximately 4,000, and in close quarters, any illness could be passed on to one another quite easily. I did not want to spend a month on a troop ship laden with horror stories of heat, sea sickness, and what-have-you. I became determined to win the position of colonel's orderly, so I studied and worked on my gear profusely. I had to be the best soldier in the battalion. It is quite comical now to think back at what I did to achieve the title of colonel's orderly. Every chance I had I would study the general orders, chain of command, the weapons manuals, as well as general soldiering. You never knew what questions would be asked of you, so you would have to memorize everything. Your weapon and appearance had to be spotless. I studied on and on, and when it came to my appearance, I put my heart and soul in getting ready. I actually had a patent leather coating I smeared on my boots after I polished and "spit shined" them for what seemed like hours. I bought a can of Niagara spray starch for my uniform. I used up the entire can on my uniform and leaned my pants up against the wall. They actually stood up by themselves. To blouse the pants legs, I used two #10 fruit cans with the top and bottom removed to put into the base of my pants legs. They formed a perfect circle around the top of my boots for a finishing touch. All the effort sure worked. The day finally came when we were ordered into formation and were inspected by the highest-ranking officers that we had ever encountered up to that day. Low and behold, I was announced the title of colonel's orderly and received two letters of commendation, one from the battalion commander and one from the brigade commander. I was also awarded the flight over to Vietnam with the advanced party and three-day passes in succession for the twenty-eight day waiting period we had before our flight would leave. The rest of the brigade left on July 15th, 1966 on the two transports. During the time I waited before my flight, my duty was to clean-up the vacated billets that my battalion left behind. During the clean-up, two forty-pound dumbbells were found that were left behind by one of the soldiers. They were given to me. We were allowed two duffel bags apiece for our clothing and personal gear to accompany us to Vietnam. I placed one dumbbell in the top of each of my duffel bags. The day we loaded them into the deuce and a half trucks, I threw mine up to a soldier up on the pile.

He exclaimed when it almost knocked him over because it was top-heavy, "Who-the-hell is taking a bowling-ball to Vietnam?" I just looked at him and had a good laugh! Every three days, I had to check back in to head-quarters while enjoying my three-day passes. On one of my passes, when I got to go home, I found out some heart-breaking news. My mother had been admitted to the Connecticut Valley Hospital diagnosed with a nervous break-down. I had a tough time easing her mind when I visited her there. I also had a very trying time accepting this for I knew it was because of my upcoming deployment. I was devastated. A few months later, while in Vietnam, I was notified and relieved that my mother was released from the hospital and returned home.

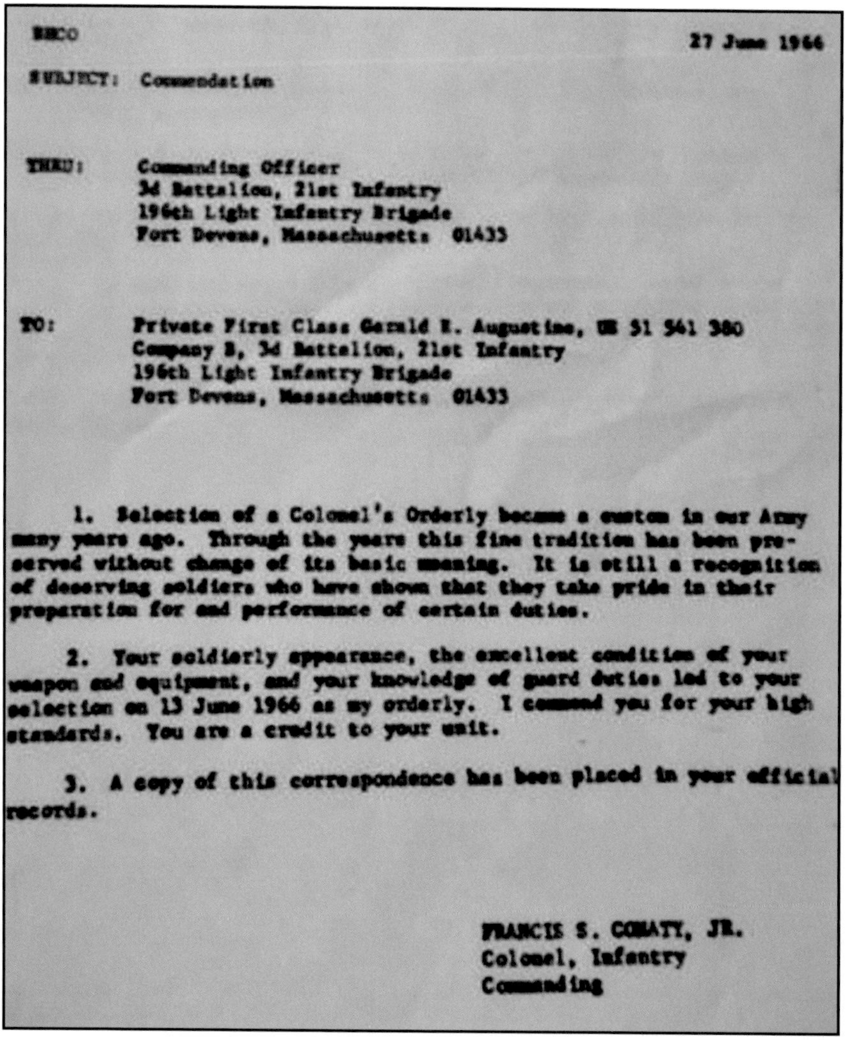

BHCO   27 June 1966

SUBJECT: Commendation

THRU: Commanding Officer
          3d Battalion, 21st Infantry
          196th Light Infantry Brigade
          Fort Devens, Massachusetts 01433

TO: Private First Class Gerald E. Augustine, US 51 561 380
          Company B, 3d Battalion, 21st Infantry
          196th Light Infantry Brigade
          Fort Devens, Massachusetts 01433

     1. Selection of a Colonel's Orderly became a custom in our Army
many years ago. Through the years this fine tradition has been pre-
served without change of its basic meaning. It is still a recognition
of deserving soldiers who have shown that they take pride in their
preparation for and performance of certain duties.

     2. Your soldierly appearance, the excellent condition of your
weapon and equipment, and your knowledge of guard duties led to your
selection on 13 June 1966 as my orderly. I commend you for your high
standards. You are a credit to your unit.

     3. A copy of this correspondence has been placed in your official
records.

                                   FRANCIS S. COHATY, JR.
                                   Colonel, Infantry
                                   Commanding

RBBCO-AUGUSTINE, Gerald E.   1st Ind
US 51 541 380 (27 Jun 66)
SUBJECT: Letter of Commendation

Headquarters, 3d Battalion, 21st Infantry, Fort Devens, Massachusetts 01433
30 June 1966

THRU: Commanding Officer, Company B, 3d Battalion, 21st Infantry, Fort
       Devens, Massachusetts 01433

TO: Private First Class Gerald E. Augustine, US 51 541 380, Company B,
       3d Battalion, 21st Infantry, Fort Devens, Massachusetts 01433

    1. It is always a great pleasure for me to receive a letter stating
that a Gimlet has done a commendable job.

    2. In addition to the Brigade Commander's comments let me assure
you that your attention to detail and preparation for other jobs in the past
have been noted and I am sure your standards will remain at this high level
in the future.

    3. A copy of this correspondence will be placed in your permanent
military record.

                            JOHN B. WADSWORTH, JR.
                            Lt Colonel, Infantry
                            Commanding

5. Marriage and Off to Nam

During the spring of '66, when most of our training was complete, I was granted a leave so I could return home to be married. We were to be married in a local Catholic Church and were taking Pre-Cana classes. My upbringing never included weekly church services or religious education, so I never received First Communion or Confirmation. I was told that I would be receiving these on my wedding day, so I was offered to take the Glencliff Correspondence Course of Catholic religious studies. I successfully completed the course and was looking forward to be married. My wedding day was May 21st, also my father's birthday. My best friend, Jim, was my best man. Everything went well, nothing out of the ordinary, but in the back of my mind, I was concerned about my upcoming time away from home as a combat infantryman. My wife was allowed to stay on post for a couple weeks prior to our deployment. The daily routine was still general soldiering and requesting passes, so the soldiers could spend more time with their families. When I was spending my three-day passes at home, I hung out with my friends at the Friendly's parking lot where all the hot cars assembled. The lot would empty out when a drag race was planned. Everyone would follow the cars for three miles just to watch the quarter mile race on a flat section of highway. It was like a caravan getting there. One such night, I was to race a new 396 powered Chevelle. My best friend Jim exited my car when we lined up on the highway. He proceeded to flag us off. We noticed a state police cruiser just on the other side of the galvanized highway dividers. Everyone left the scene as fast as they were able, including myself. I made it home late that night, not knowing whatever happened to my friend Jim. I was worried. The following morning, I was told by Jim that when everyone left him stranded, the state trooper motioned him over to his cruiser and arrested him. He had a court date in about a month to face charges of "illegal use of the highway by a pedestrian." We never forgot that night. Most nights spent were pretty similar with a lot of mischief going on. When my deployment was getting closer, I put my '40 Ford up on blocks in my friend Jim's aunt's garage. I began to go around to my friends and family, saying goodbyes and letting them know that I wouldn't be around for a while. Back at the base on July 15th, I helped my company load up their gear and saw them off to Boston where they would board the two transports and be on their way to Vietnam. I still had until August 2nd, when I would be transported to Edwards Air Force base to board a jetliner with the advanced party of mostly officers and be on my way to join my battalion in Nam. With a blink of an eye it seemed, August 2nd was there. We flew from Camp Edwards to Elmendorf Air Force Base in Alaska on a Saturday and slept overnight at the airfield. I awoke on Sunday morning to a beautiful sunrise highlighting snowcapped mountain peaks off in the distance. After a wonderful breakfast, we boarded our aircraft and were off to Yakota air base in Japan for refueling. This is the first time I learned how much better officers were treated than "grunts," which is what I happened to be. The time at Yakota was only used for refueling. Before we knew it, we were on our way to Tan Son Nhut air base near Saigon, the capitol of South Vietnam. When we arrived, it was close to midnight on August 4th. I will never forget the heat and humidity when that door opened up and I stepped off into that God forsaken climate of my new home for 365 days. It was in the high nineties. I was abruptly transported to a one-story warehouse on the base where I slept on a crude bunkbed amongst other newbies, not knowing where I was headed to next. "Not knowing" was very common to the member of a squad of a rifle platoon. Our job was to kill the enemy, protect your fellow soldier, and obey the orders that are given you no matter what they are. My most important mission was to stay alive for another day. Welcome to the life of a combat infantryman.

AUTHOR, ONE MONTH BEFORE DEPLOYMENT

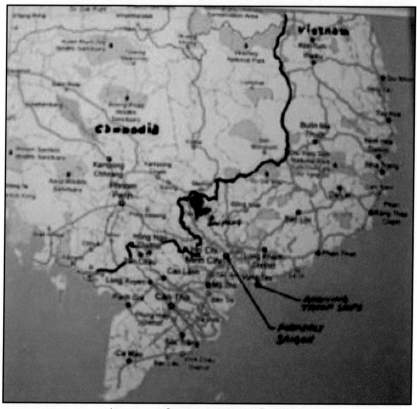

LANDED IN SAIGON—NEXT STOP TAY NINH

6. Tay Ninh Base Camp

I woke up on my first morning in Nam at the Tan Son Nhut air base. I folded up my dress uniform and placed it in my duffel bag. I got dressed into my jungle fatigues that I would be wearing for the next twelve months. When I stepped out of the warehouse to go for breakfast at the mess hall, I immediately noticed the smell of rancid air. The heat and humidity didn't help matters. After a hearty army breakfast, I was directed to be at the airstrip to board a C130 transport plane that would fly me and the advanced party northwest fifty-five miles to Tay Ninh Province where I would wait for the rest of my unit to arrive. The flight did not take long. This is when I learned that everything from here on in would be "bare-bones." Nothing what-so-ever that we were used to at home. The plane shook and swerved almost like being on a carnival ride. I had to hang on when we landed, or I would have been abruptly thrown forward and injured. When I stepped off the plane with my duffel bag, I found myself in a true war zone. We landed in a deep, muddy short strip that you could tell that was recently cleared. It was to be used for C-130's and choppers, which could land and take off in very short distances. I looked around and noticed soldiers from the 25th Infantry Division (tropic lightning) who were securing the area with their reconnaissance party while also waiting for the 196th to arrive. I also noticed in the distance a high mountain that looked out of place in this flat land. It was called Nui Ba-Den, or "Black Virgin Mountain." According to the story passed down over the years, it was named after a dark-skinned Cambodian girl who wandered up the mountain and was attacked and killed by a tiger.

I arrived during monsoon season. Every day at approximately 4 P.M., very dark clouds moved in and opened up with torrential downpours. When I arrived at this location, I received a pup tent and cot and instructions to set up on the edge of the air strip. I was also told where to walk to get my chow three times a day. I learned then that my unit wouldn't be arriving for about ten more days. While I was waiting for my buddies, the downpours were so fierce that I had a stream flowing under my cot. Choppers (slicks), C130's, and some gun-ships landed and took off day and night. Occasionally a larger C-47 (Chinook, two rotor helicopter) would show up. One more thing I have to mention that happened on my first day there. I looked up at a Huey and noticed a body dangling from some sort of rope. I questioned the closest soldier what was going on. He responded that the person hanging from the chopper was a South Vietnamese soldier, an interpreter, and suspected spy. He would be dropped if he didn't talk. Needless to say, it frightened the Hell out of me, and I became sick to my stomach. I looked up to the sky and said to myself, *What the hell am I doing here?* I vividly remember that to this day. I think back to this time while waiting for my unit that I didn't have to go out on any missions with the 25th. Thank God for that. During the wait one afternoon, I heard a chopper right over my little tent. I looked up and saw a small helicopter with a round plexiglass bubble-type canopy in the front. Before I knew it, it landed not twenty-five feet away from me. The commanding officers from the 25th approached it abruptly. Who should step out but General Westmoreland. I was in such awe that I didn't even take my camera out and take a photo. Before I could get my wits about me, he finished up his business and was on his way.

BUILDING THE BASE CAMP

It was a happy reunion when my buddies finally showed up and we began to build the Tay Ninh base camp. The previous ten months together, we became very close. We were like brothers. We immediately got into a scheduled pattern of rotating duties between the various companies, platoons, and squads. For the first month of our combat tour, our main mission was to build the Tay Ninh base camp. It was to be on a huge tract of land just outside the city and not far from the base of Nui Ba-Den Mountain. The mission of the 196th Light Infantry Brigade was to stop the infiltrating of the North Vietnam Army and Viet Cong coming down the Ho-Chi-Minh trail and Cambodian border heading to Saigon, the capital city of South Vietnam. During the day, the weather was like a desert, hot, dry, and dusty. You couldn't drink enough water, it was over 100 degrees, and your clothing was always wet with sweat. Our "home," tents, or" hootches" went up pretty rapidly. They would become a welcomed site when returning from extended combat missions or just to get out of the brutal sun when you were relieved from other duties. A wooden raised floor, a bunk, and foot locker was a welcomed site. Another daily chore was building the perimeter bunkers around the whole base camp. All day was spent in the direct sun filling hundreds upon hundreds of sand bags that were then placed over a skeleton frame of eight-by-eight-inch beams. They were built to repel or protect you from small arms fire, mortar, R.P.G. (rifle propelled grenades), and other explosive devices. The routine of "bunker line duty" had already begun from the start of building the base camp. There was perimeter security 24/7 on a rotating basis by all the rifle platoons on post. Usually there were three men per position, so you would be on watch for one hour and then have two hours of sleep through the night. The newly finished bunkers became a welcomed site. Believe me, when I was out on bunker line through the night, I never would sleep in those bunkers. During my break, I would sleep on the hard ground about fifteen meters to the rear of them. To me they were a target. Any sapper could throw a satchel charge or grenade into one of the windows or doors or just come storming through the door with a barking AK-47. Many other duties had to be performed to make the base camp productive. Some of these were: K.P. duty, or kitchen police, burning of the excrement, or stirring the human waste mixed in with kerosene. The latter was the most undesirable duty to be on while in base camp. So many guys tried to get out of that duty using every excuse possible. Most excuses didn't work, the sergeants had heard them all. Also tending to one's gear on a daily basis was on everyone's list. Still the best times had were spent in the base camp. Right from the beginning while the base camp was being built, combat missions were carried on fighting the VC 9th division, in and around war zone "C," where we were located. Operation Attleboro had just begun, which was the first multi-battalion operation of the war and was to be the biggest battle in the war so far. Since we were "newbies," most of our duty while the camp was being built was directed upon inside the grounds of the camp or security around the perimeter. All around the perimeter, there were layers upon layers of stranded barbed wire supported by wooden sticks. The gates were made of a pole frame meshed with strands of barb wire. I remember my first night in particular when four of us were assigned to one of the main gates to the compound. We were to be there overnight, rotating sleeping times through the night and would sleep on the ground nearby. We remained in our fatigues and kept our weapons at the ready. One of the guys had a brainstorm of wanting to get his Jolley's off. There was a local hootch only about a hundred feet from our post. His idea was to go out one by one and get taken care of. The cost was fifty cents. It didn't sound like a good idea to me, but when it came to my turn, I didn't want to be a prude so I followed their directions and ended up in the hutch, the size of a small garage. I paid the fee to this woman that I was told later was sixty-two. There was a single candle there giving off a dull, flickering glow. When the woman smiled, all I could see was dark brown stubs for teeth. Her skin was so tanned and wrinkled, it looked like tomatoes that were left in the sun for days making paste. I leaned my back against the wall, still holding on to my rifle, and periodically nodded to her graciously while she nodded back until I thought it was time to leave and my buddies would think I was taken care of.

First Ambush

When the bunkers were finally completed around the perimeter, our platoon sergeants began to take us out on ambush patrols, one of the most dreaded duties an infantryman has to partake in. Every day predetermined positions were established for a night ambush patrol to be set up. Suspected enemy routes or known enemy activity would become the prime location for an ambush. To this day, I remember going on my first ambush. It was also the first time I left the base camp to be out in the boonies overnight. Most ambushes I accompanied were squad sized or about six to eight men. Some were two squad sized or even platoon sized. I averaged about two ambushes a week or 100 of them during my combat tour. An R.T.O. (Radio telephone operator) would always accompany an ambush patrol, along with the squad leader, riflemen, grenadiers, and on occasion, an M-60 machine gun team. We lined up at dusk, my platoon Sgt. Ronald S. Figueroa would take us out, a squad sized ambush patrol. His R.T.O., my machine gun team, two grenadiers (M79), and two riflemen made up this patrol. We each had a claymore mine that would be set up to the front of each position. I cannot describe the feeling I had in the pit of my stomach when I was standing there lined up, getting ready to leave the base camp. There were other patrols going out at the same time. There was actually a Priest there dressed in white, standing over a portable table giving Holy Communion. I noticed some of the other soldiers were praying in their own way. When I saw this scene, I wondered if I would be coming back. We glanced at each other and noticed a look we had never seen before on each other's faces. It was a form of horror. During my time in Nam, the feelings never changed.

CLAYMORE MINE SAFETY

While spending time in base camp the first month, bad news traveled fast. A soldier in "A" company, not too far from our "B" company, was demonstrating the use of a claymore mine to a new recruit. He was showing him the proper use for an upcoming ambush patrol. He explained the device should be placed at least ten to twelve meters to the front and have the arch facing forward. While showing him how to arm the weapon, he placed the detonator on his cot. He proceeded to install the blasting cap into the orifice. Someone picked up the detonator and squeezed it, setting off the mine. A soldier walking by the tent was killed. The recruit standing in the aisle lost both legs to his knees, landed on his stumps, and rolled over. Word was immediately passed that detonators would only be placed in claymores at the ambush sites.

TAY NINH BASE CAMP PERIMETER W/ M60
NUI BA-DEN MOUNTAIN

PATROL OUTSIDE BASE CAMP

PERIMETER BUNKERS AT TAY NINH BASE CAMP

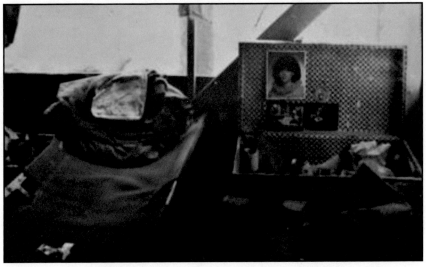

MY COT AT "HOME BASE" WITH FORTY-POUND DUMBELLS

MY FIRST NIGHT IN NAM-CAMP ALPHA

MY FIRST BREAKFAST IN NAM

Local vendors at Camp Alpha, Tan-Son-Nhut air base

Author preparing for ambush

AUTHOR AT TAY NINH BASE CAMP

PHOTO FROM
"NAM — THE VIETNAM EXPERIENCE 1965 — 1975"
BARNES & NOBLE BOOKS

7. First Missions

THE MILLION DOLLAR WOUND

This happened during my first few weeks in Nam. While the base camp was still being developed, we began to leave on daylight patrols searching the region in close proximity to our base. This was done on a rotating basis with other platoons and would take the monotony out of filling sandbags all day and spending time in the open sun guarding the perimeter. On this particular mission, my platoon lined up at the main gate near our company headquarters. It was nearing a hundred degrees. After checking one another out to see if our gear was up to par, we headed down the main road away from camp and the city. We made sure we kept our distance with one another and not to bunch up. We were always taught that it was better to lose one of us than a group all at once. This was common sense. Eventually we trudged through a small, thick wood line and came upon an expansive rice paddy. We spread out abreast of one another, at least ten meters, and began to cross the paddy. I was to the right of my squad leader, Sgt. John Carvalho. We began to approach the edge of the paddy and the beginning of a tree-line. All of a sudden, in front of us, about twenty meters away, emerged a VC out of a "spider-hole," and "pop" went his carbine, a distinct sound that you could tell what weapon it was. Sarge doubled over as I dove to the ground. The ground was hard and dry and not what you would expect a rice paddy to be, being in the monsoon season. The VC soldier disappeared through an exit to the rear of his enclave, and no one returned fire. The VC used this form of engagement often. Just one shot could put a whole company of men down. We brought the medic up, and I helped prepare the sarge to be extricated by placing his poncho under him and carrying him to the arriving medevac chopper for a "dust-off." The sarge's tour was over. We later found out that the round went through one of his canteens and into his hip and wasn't life threatening. It sent him home. The term "million -dollar wound" was heard throughout the camp the next few days. A million-dollar wound meant that you got to go home alive and is worth a million dollars to you. Would you rather have a million dollars or your life?

THE WELL

Another close call that took place during my first few weeks of my one-year tour happened on my first ambush patrol. Sgt. Ronald Figueroa, our platoon Sergeant, took two squads of our platoon out by compass to a predetermined ambush site. It was a half mile from base camp. In most cases, we would stay off trails and roads. We didn't want to be in "Charlie's" gun sites and be a victim of his ambush. It was a little past dusk, and Sgt. "Fig" had it on his mind to bring us to the site unscathed and return in the same condition. We all looked up to him as he was experienced and did everything right to protect our butts and always had the thought in his mind to bring us back alive. We trusted him. It was dark that night, and I remember Sgt. Fig stating that we should travel through the back yards of the local hootches in order to stay off the beaten paths. It was hot and humid as usual, so wiping sweat and slapping mosquitoes was the norm. We brought along the minimum of gear with us, so we could travel light and fast. It still amounted to about thirty-five pounds per man. Two canteens of water, your weapon, along with 200 rounds of ammo packed into your web-gear, three or four hand grenades, helmet, and bayonet. We usually carried a bandolier of M-60 machine-gun ammo per rifleman, too. Of course the sergeant's R.T.O. had the twenty-five-pound PRC-25 radio with him. As we approached the back of the hamlets, we could hear a cluck or two from the dodging chickens and an occasional groan from a water buffalo. The thick grass was nearly a half foot high, and the palms and shrubbery native to the area was scattered thinly throughout the yards. To the rear of the yards lay thicker shrubbery as it was up against the edge of a wood-line. No sign of a resident anywhere as there was a strict curfew in affect, so no one was to be out and about after dark. I guarantee they knew we were there. After about fifteen minutes of navigating through the difficult terrain of weeds, grass, and plantings, the earth came out from under me. I fell right down into a backyard well. I threw my rifle to the side to protect it as I began flailing my arms. Lucky Sgt. Fig was close to me as he reached down with his rifle-butt to pull me up. I was under water as I reached up to feel the rifle stock while sinking quickly with that heavy weight attached to me. As he pulled me up, he grabbed the harness to my web-gear and was able to extricate me. After the shock wore off and some muffled laughter, we were on our way to set up the ambush. Needless to say, I was very uncomfortable all night being soaked, full of bugs and such, and smelling like a sewer. While I stayed awake all night, the best occurrence of all was that no VC crossed our path.

THE ISLAND

Our turn came up to go out on a platoon sized ambush patrol. All during the day, while we attended to our base camp duties, we thought about what we would face that evening. It wasn't normal protocol to have a full-size platoon go out, usually a squad or two. We all lined up at one of the gates just before dusk. Those wishing a short religious service were accommodated by a chaplain. Business as usual took over the mood as we checked out each other's gear. We headed out in single file eventually crossing a huge dried up rice paddy about a mile from camp. In the center of this huge patch of ground was an island of trees and growth about the size of a baseball diamond. Our platoon leader spread the word that this was a good a place as any to set up our ambush. We immediately circled the plot and entered its perimeter and began to set up our NDP's. Claymores were set out as we requested to have three-man positions, so we could get two hours of sleep for every one hour on watch. It wasn't to be. Two-man positions was the call. There was not enough manpower to provide three-man positions; we would have been spread out too thin. It was to be a tough night, one hour on watch, one hour asleep all through the night. One thing about these ambushes and NDPs, you become a very patient individual. While staring out into the darkness, there is plenty of time to reminisce about your past and to dream about what your future will be like. Another hot and humid night in the Nam was to be as we slept in our stinky, wet fatigues, whacking the bugs and mosquitoes off. One of my turns on watch was from 4 to 5 A.M. I was abruptly woken for it as my buddy dove to the ground and passed out, taking in his much-needed sleep. We all reacted this way. Fifteen minutes into this watch, we were alerted that there was movement coming our way. We whispered just loud enough so the next position would be alerted. Claymore activation devises were picked up and at the ready. The next communication we heard was that it was only a farmer coming through accompanied by his single water buffalo. There was a curfew in affect; he was not supposed to be out at that hour. Everyone held their composure. The farmer approached right by my position. I don't know what got into me, but I reached out with my arm as the water buffalo walked past. I scraped his hide with my hand all the way down his side. It was hot and soaking wet and stunk. I am so glad he didn't react. We let the farmer go on his way. He never knew we were there and never realized he was so close to being blown away.

WATER BUFFALO AND FARMER

MEDEVAC HUEY (UH-1)

SOUTH VIETNAMESE VILLAGE FAMILY - NOTE: NO YOUNG MEN

Village "hootch"

8. Base Camp Completed

When the base camp was completed, we began to participate more in search and destroy missions in and around Tay Ninh province known as war zone "C." We were located fifty-five miles northwest of Saigon, close to the Cambodian border. Our main mission was to defray the infiltration from the VC 9th Division, 272nd, and 273rd regiments. They were coming down through the Ho-Chi-Minh trail, which ran along the Cambodian border and through Laos. They were also hiding their stashes deep into the forests of Cambodia. At the time, we were ordered not to bomb or fight in Cambodia. We were deep into operation Attleboro, working along with the 25th Infantry Division who were fighting the 272nd VC regiment. In five days of fighting, 758 dead VC were actual body count statistics. There were many more dragged off by their compatriots. Among the recovered goods from the enemy, 1,000 tons of rice were hauled out by the 196th and distributed to the south Vietnamese populace. We came upon caches of stacked rice on hand-built pallets six inches above ground to protect it from the elements. Many of the 100-pound sacks had CARE stamped on them, which baffled the heck out of us. Where did the rice originate? We proceeded to place all the rice on the heavy-duty Chinook choppers and some even on tanks and APCs (armored personnel carriers). You have to remember, most of the fighting took place in the jungle where the VC could easily hide and couldn't be spotted from the air. He mostly would hit at night, he dreaded facing our superior fire power. Many times we searched out areas that had been sprayed with herbicides (defoliants), as there was no vegetation in the tree-tops. Agent Orange was the most common we witnessed, as they were packaged in bright orange drums. If the VC happened to filter into the villages, it was our job to rout them out. It was very rare that they would face us in the daylight. A mission that comes to mind was when our company was to relieve units of the 25th infantry division. It was during Operation Attleboro just after a major battle they had near the Ho-Chi-Minh trail. It was the first two weeks of November. The 1st Infantry Division (Big Red One) was called in to assist. For three days, dead American G.I.s from the B.R.O. were unable to be extricated from the battle zone. My platoon had the duty of carrying out the thirty plus bodies to be put into body bags and place on the choppers to be sent back to base. I've never seen such a horrible sight in my life. The bodies were stiff like plastic manikins. I was horrified when I saw a major's head that had his eye socket completely blown out. That night we were ordered to set up NDPs at the same location where the bodies were extricated from. It wasn't a pretty site. There were so many of us that most of us had to dig our own fox-holes. It was one of the worst nights I had in Nam up to that point. First of all, no one should ever witness a fresh battle scene. Most of the trees were blown away, two to six feet above ground. There were holes of all sizes in the ground everywhere around us. Flies were buzzing throughout over the blood-soaked earth. There were a few carcasses of deer and other animals familiar with Vietnam. The worst thing of all was the horrific stench of the smell of death. It is the most grotesque smell of rotten flesh, especially that the corpses laid there in hundred-degree heat for three days. Guys in my unit were puking as they were digging in while setting up their defensive position. It was no place to be. Some of the digging was tough going. You couldn't get beyond the roots of some of the trees. By dusk all of our positions were supposed to be ready. Some of us found the digging so difficult, we ended up laying prone in one-foot trenches. Field of fire orders were given to everyone. Charlie was expected to return. Some were to fire ground level, others at standing height, and a few into the trees, what was left of them. We rotated sleeping times, so there was always one awake per position throughout the night, if one could sleep at all. Deep into the night, all hell broke loose. Our support teams fired parachute flares over our position, and as they floated earthward, it became as bright as day. This caused strange moving shadows to envelope the surroundings. Everyone opened up with their weapons as instructed. We repelled the enemy as I don't think a flea could've gotten through the firepower we put out. We were thrilled to leave this area in the morning with no casualties on our side.

STAND-DOWN

We returned from the bush for a much-needed break to wash-up, tend to our gear, write letters, and enjoy the pleasantries of just being in base camp. Your chance of going home in a body-bag was much less. Beer was always in abundance at the rec tent where you could play cards, write letters, snack on what was sent from home, or just be with your buddies. If you were into "pot," it was readily available in town or at the perimeter where the locals, mostly young girls, would sell it to you through the barbed wire. It was comical to see the pot heads get the hungries. They would low-crawl in the dark to the mess tent and steal cases of C-rations from under the tent flaps. They would put them on their back and low-crawl back to the rec tent and fight over their favorite individual meals. There seemed to always be a division between the pot-heads and the beer drinkers. We still had to take our turns burning shit, being on K.P., guarding the perimeter, and going out on ambush-patrols. This is where I met my good friend, Wayne Lizotte, a short- timer from another rifle platoon. He noticed that I had some weights that I brought along, so while we were on perimeter security, we were able to work-out together. We even built an exercise bench out of sandbags and concocted a barbell out of a bamboo pole with sandbags tied to the ends. He told me to look him up when I returned to the states as he only lived in Springfield, Massachusetts, only about forty miles from where I lived. He told me about body-building contests they held at Mountain Park in Holyoke, Massachusetts because he thought that I had potential to become a competitor someday. Times spent at base camp was short lived as we always had to be ready for a mission, which were getting more prevalent as time went on.

NVA/VC – TONS OF RICE

HAULING OUT TONS OF RICE TO BE EXTRICATED

"POT" GIRLS AT THE PERIMETER

NVA/VC RICE TO BE SENT TO FRIENDLY LINES

AUTHOR PHOTOGRAPHED TANKS DURING BATTLE
NOTE VC BICYCLE

ARMOR UNITS WERE THERE WHEN NEEDED

9. The Daily Grind

A NEW WEAPON

When we arrived in Vietnam, we were so used to the M14 rifle. It was our baby for the previous ten months. We did everything with her. We earned our expert marksmanship badge, took her to guard duty, and practiced riot control. Remember we were supposed to be shipped to Santo Domingo for police action. We marched with her for hours on end while training and in parades. We went through many inspections and were able to disassemble and put her back in operable condition with our eyes closed. We never got to be re-associated with this fine weapon in Nam. We were issued something we knew nothing about. It was the M16 Armalite Assault Rifle. It was a compact, light-weight weapon, which became the standard issue with the U. S. forces in Vietnam. It was cal. 5.56 mm, 39.6 inches in length, and weighed 6.37 pounds empty. We happened to be the Guinea pigs to overcome the teething problems it had right from the beginning. We never even got to fire it before going on our first missions or ambush patrols. Many soldiers were found dead with their cleaning rods out, trying to eject the jammed spent cartridge, the only round they got to fire in battle. When I fired my first round, the spent cartridge was found stuck in the chamber with its ejecting rim chipped off. This I find criminal on the part of the manufacturer. Here we were fighting for our lives, and we were supplied with malfunctioning equipment. While testing was further accomplished, it was found that the slow burning ball powder ammunition was notorious for leaving calcium carbonate deposits in the gas tube. When this occurred, the M16 jammed instantly. Also, the climate had an effect on the chambers, which would corrode. They had to be redesigned and chromed, which alleviated the problem. One more thing, when using thirty round magazines, it was found that the magazine spring was too weak and would cause jamming. When these issues were finally corrected, the M16 evolved into a formidable weapon. In 1963, when Colt Firearms Corporation took over production, they supplied the army with 85,000 M16's. The next three years, they supplied them with 200,000 more. You would think that the problems we encountered would have been ironed out before putting our young men in harm's way.

Jungle Rot

Being out in the field in this hundred-degree weather, sweating profusely, constantly being wet and dirty took its toll on many of us. A friend of mine from Farmington, Connecticut, Carl, had rashes and open sores on his lower legs so bad that he became the battalion PX clerk throughout his whole tour. I became affected with jungle rot on my penis and tried to self-treat it with over-the-counter ointments. It was embarrassing, so I held off seeing the medics until it progressively got worse. I finally complained and was sent to see a Dr. Rose at a military hospital compound. While waiting my turn to see the doctor, I noticed a shocking sight. A soldier was submerged in a large tub of ice cubes with only his head above the surface. I questioned the nearest medic as to what had happened. I was told the soldier was sleeping against the tracks of a tank when it abruptly drove off. The soldier was dragged by barbed-wire through some fuel cans, which ignited and became burned to a great degree. It was humbling to behold. I explained to Dr. Rose my symptoms. He mixed up a paste of penicillin and talcum powder and told me to keep on applying the potion until it healed. It was important that I kept applying more talc to keep myself dry because fungus thrives in dark, moist areas. I am happy to say the prescription served the trick, and I healed up in no time. Many years later, I was reading a periodical about Vietnam and Dr. Rose was mentioned. I learned that he was the most famous doctor that served during the Vietnam war.

MULE

When not using the slicks for transportation, we would just rough it most of the time hunting Charlie and his stashes of weapons and food. Being the strongest man in the company had its drawbacks. Not only did I not have the fun of the grab-ass games as I was always avoided, I became the "mule" on the forced marches and extended company patrols. When the company had to relocate to a new area to work out of, the mortar platoon naturally had to join us. I was chosen often to carry the thirty-five-pound base plate of the 3.5 mortar. It was strapped to my back in addition to my thirty-five pounds of combat gear. Just try carrying seventy pounds of gear all day long in a 100-degree plus steaming climate. Many times at the end of the day, when we set up our NDP, I would fall onto my back like a turtle, soaking wet, unable to roll over. My buddies had to help me out of my gear. I remember being so sore that it would take me all night to recuperate.

CLOSE ENCOUNTERS

Being new soldiers in Nam wasn't easy. We would look up to the "short-timers" (guys with little time left in their tour), constantly asking for advice and would listen attentively to their war stories. No matter what they told us, we would believe them. I remember one night we were positioned amongst a platoon of APC's and tanks. Now these guys were experienced or so it seemed. Either they were showing off to us newbies or they spent a little too much time living in the jungle dodging bullets. We heard from them that if you survived the first thirty days of your tour, you would have a good chance of making it home. We also learned from them to always lay low, hug the ground, and keep your steel pot on. We had a new replacement platoon leader join our company, Lt. Robert Brockman, who didn't abide by the advice given. His first week in country, he made the extreme sacrifice. While on one of our patrols, he stood up tall, and a sniper round found its mark and killed him. This proved the point of what we had been told. From then on, many of us abided by the "rules of jungle warfare" more closely. While we were working with the armor unit, one night, a tanker was perched up on his turret scanning the jungle in front of him. He was looking through his infra-red scope mounted on his fifty-caliber machine gun. He spotted an NVA soldier standing with his bicycle next to a tree lighting up a smoke. The tanker let the "50" rip. The Charlie never knew what hit him; he exploded into hundreds of pieces. Another close encounter to a body bag that I should mention happened to me. We were on a company sized search and destroy mission. We were far out into the "boonies," somewhere we hadn't been before. The landscape was fairly barren, similar to a desert scene you see in a western movie. We were approaching a low hill, only about twenty feet in height. Through communication from the forward observers, an old abandoned village, or so they thought, was spotted beyond the hill. The company commander and his associates decided it was a wise move to put the company on line and attack the village. As we were charging up the hill, I disappeared from site. I fell into a wide hole, which was about five feet in diameter and about four feet deep. It was covered with thin branches and growth common to the surrounding area. It is commonly known as a "Pungi-pit" in jungle warfare jargon. Pungi-pits were used extensively throughout the Vietnam war. Even before the occupation of American forces, they were used. The idea came from the trapping of animals, which were used for thousands of years. These human traps are dug into the ground at varying sizes, most being four to six feet deep and from two to four feet in diameter. Bamboo stakes are usually stuck vertically into the bottom of the hole with the tips sharpened to a fine point. At times human excrement was placed on the tips in order to cause infection to the victims who happen to fall into the trap. We were issued jungle boots, which had steel plates built into the soles, so the stakes wouldn't penetrate our feet. Luckily for me, this pit had been there for quite some time. The vertical bamboo stakes were rotted and beyond use for what they were intended for. When my body landed on them, they just collapsed under me as fate was on my side. I crawled out of that hole pretty shaken up, got my senses together, and continued on the mission. Another one of our lucky encounters, the village was totally abandoned.

DEALING WITH THE LOCALS

Being out in the boonies for days on end was a common occurrence. Searching for Charlie was the priority of course. Some days when we checked out villages and interrogated the locals, I would try to make friends, especially the children.

I became good at speaking common Vietnamese phrases. I carried a Vietnamese to English-English to Vietnamese booklet with me and studied it every chance I had the time. Upon entering a village or just running into the populace, I would immediately draw the people to me when I spoke a catchy phrase. I became a conversation piece to them as they thought I spoke their language fluently. To me it was fun. To find something fun in this God-forsaken place was out of the ordinary. I continued to study and learn more phrases. At different times we would enter a village, and I would call out a phrase and some villagers would bring me ice water or soda. The other soldiers always wondered what I was saying to be rewarded this special treatment. At times I was brought up to the front to the commander to help out with the interrogation process. The most fun I got out of it was with the local children. One day, on a company sized search and destroy mission, we came upon a wooden bridge at a fork in the road. The command was at a standstill and undecided which way to head next. It was blasting hot around noon, and when we saw the pooled water under the bridge, we begged our platoon leader for the opportunity to go for a swim. We were to be there for a good half hour, so reluctantly he gave a few of us permission. A group of about twelve children from a local friendly village just happened to gather around. About six of us took all our gear and clothes off, except our trousers. When I spoke to the children in Vietnamese, they became instantly friendly. They jumped in the water, which looked like liquid chocolate. That's how muddy it was. Being very strong, I was able to "shot-put" the children into the air like a catapult. They absolutely loved the adventure and kept on coming back for more. That and the catchy phrases made me sort of a hero to them. It was very enjoyable. Unfortunately it was short lived, and we had to move on. When I got out of the water to get dressed, I found that I was covered with about twenty-five leeches all over my body. Their heads were already burrowed into my skin. They were even dug into my scrotum. My squad leader, Sgt. Moke (Mokalahua), our Hawaiian Sgt., used a burning cigarette tip and some insect repellant to coax them out. If you pulled them off, the heads would break off and you could become seriously infected. The children were giggling as this was taking place. To them dealing with leeches must be very common and doesn't bother them one bit.

CREATURES

Another creature we weren't fond of was fire ants. They were everywhere. One day, while stopping for a "C" ration lunch while on a mission, I happened to sit next to a tree. I didn't notice the red fire ants and shot up screaming in pain. It felt like hypodermic needles sticking me in my butt. We were always on constant watch for them, as well as other nasty creatures common to the Nam. We were also warned about banded viper snakes. These were snakes about a foot or two long that had alternating one-inch bands of brown and off-white markings. They were so deadly, we were told, that if you get bitten, you would only get to walk three steps, then you would die. I never wanted to be tested. I did get to see some vipers that some soldiers killed and was happy to never confront any live ones.

OPERATIONS

The most famous operation, the 196th, was noted for was operation Attleboro. The first multi-battalion operation of the war. The seventy-two-day operation resulted in 1,106 dead from the 9th VC Division, with the cost of 155 dead and 800 wounded Americans. A thousand-ton of rice and twenty-five tons of salt was captured. Now that operation Attleboro had ended on November 24th, 1966, the 196th became involved in operation Cedar Falls. Its purpose was to drive the Viet Cong out of the Iron Triangle. The Iron Triangle was a forty-square-mile communist sanctuary, just north of Saigon, controlled by the VC. This operation lasted until January 26th, 1967. It resulted in 2,700 acres of cleared jungle by stepped up spraying of Agent Orange. Five-hundred tunnels and 1,100 bunkers were destroyed. Seven-hundred-fifty confirmed enemy dead at a cost of seventy-two American lives. From there the 196th became involved with operation Gadsden that lasted from February 2nd to February 20th, 1967. It was planned to be a deceptive operation involving the 25th Infantry Division deployed around Lo Go City to the west. The last operation, the 196th was involved with before moving north in the beginning of March, was Junction City. It began on February 22nd, 1967 and was to be the largest operational thrust of the entire war. This operation utilized twenty-two battalions as the attacking force. This huge force was supported by seventeen artillery battalions and over 4,000 Air Force sorties. An aerial armada consisting of 249 helicopters were flown in this assault. This number remains today as the largest U.S. Army accrued assault ever undertaken, never again duplicated during this conflict or any future American assault in any war. Junction City, Phase I, II, and III. Lasted until May 14th, 1967.

AUTHOR W/ VILLAGE CHILDREN

My "B" Company, 2nd platoon 196th L.I.B. 3/21 returning from extended mission

Mounting slicks for an assault

NVA TRANSPORT MATERIALS FOUND

SEARCHING VILLAGES FOR VC AND/OR WEAPONS

SPEAKING VIETNAMESE PHRASES WHILE SEARCHING VILLAGES

AUTHOR MAKING FRIENDS

AUTHOR WITH M-16

ROBERTS AND MULDOON READY FOR COMBAT ASSAULT IN SLICK

10. Mail Call

During the last week of October '66, I was approached by our company executive officer. He notified me with a letter from the Red Cross that I had become a father of a boy on October 26th. Deep feelings came over me. I was elated and confused all at once. Would I ever get to see my son? When I received word from my wife that she named him Gerald, after me, I thought to myself, *Is that a premonition?*

BAD NEWS TRAVELS FAST

The bright side of every day, in most cases, was mail call. A letter or package from home was always a spark to keep moral high and bring a feeling of hope and caring to the soldier. When your name was called during the handouts of the mail drop, there was a feeling of goodness inside and an instant thought that the news would be good and would cheer you up. Every once in a while, there was news from home that everyone would dread. It changed the nature of the soldier, his performance, and sadly it would affect his fellow comrades. One such letter affected yours truly. It came from my mom in November of '66 while my wife and son were staying at my parents' house while I was completing my tour. In the letter was the news that every soldier dreads. My best friend was seeing my wife. I became totally humiliated, angry, and saddened. It changed my outlook of my purpose of soldiering. I wanted out of this whole mess. Many thoughts raced through my mind. I wanted to go home and kill "Jody." I lost my self-esteem and my ambition to do the best I was able to do to help my comrades get out of this hell and make it home in one piece. It took me a while to mellow out and reform. I still had nine more months of suffering in this heat, filth, stink, and witnessing trauma that no one on earth should witness in one's life-time. Not to mention the constant thought on my mind when the next bullet, booby-trap, rocket, pungi-pit, explosion, mine, or disease would take my life away. I had the chance of going home early. We were losing officers quite regularly. I was offered the opportunity, by head-quarters company, to return to the world and attend officer's candidate school, or O.C.S. for short. I questioned what the requirements were. I would have to serve an additional two years of active duty. With all that was going on in my life now, I just wanted to complete my remaining nine months, so I refused the offer. Many times we had to be counselors to our buddies when they received a disheartening letter from home. Once in a while, when cleaning our weapons or settling down at our NDPs, the counseling would take place. There was always talk of the easy way home. Mostly it was to shoot one's trigger finger off by "accident." I saw many of my buddies point a .45 caliber pistol at their fingers or at their toes. We would talk each other out of it. It would have only gotten them a few years in military prison.

HONG CONG

At about this time, I was ready to put in for my much-needed rest and recreation, or R & R as the Army called it. It hurt that I had been let down by my wife and best friend. It became a necessity that I get away to ponder over my thoughts. I was granted the trip to Hong Cong for four days along with a friend from my platoon. It was a pleasant experience touring the city and dining on the famous floating restaurant in Kowloon harbor. I also had dinner with the owner's daughter of the Presidential Hotel where I was staying. We took a liking for one another and corresponded by mail when I returned to my unit. I followed the crowd of the other grunts who were on R & R and purchased a tailored suit that was completed over night. It was a shark-skin suit along with a vest for the measly sum of $27. Another thing that was popular to bring back to your platoon was a colorful tattoo or two. I went out on a limb and brought back four. When we entered the tattoo parlor, Pinky's of Hong Cong, the first thing handed to you was a bottle of beer on the house.

It was a way to loosen you up, so you would buy more tattoos. I sort of chuck-led when I saw one of my buddies have a large rebel flag tattooed on his fore-arm. I thought what my friend, Wayne, told me about pursuing a career in body-building when I returned home and that tattoos were a distraction in judging. I am glad I followed his advice and had gotten only hidden ones. They ended up on my ass, my crotch, my big toe, and under my left arm pit. I was sort of a hero for a day when I arrived back in my squad, especially when they saw the lipstick kiss on my ass when we showered. There is another thing about R & R that is common knowledge. The percentage of young servicemen that seek out fulfillment of their carnal needs is 90 percent plus. On one particular night, I was invited to join a group of soldiers who were lined up in a hallway of my hotel. They were waiting their turn to enter a room to get their needs taken care of by a hired Asian damsel. I didn't want my needs to be satisfied in that form. I returned to my room and got some much-needed z's.

AUTHOR ON THE WAY TO HONG KONG FOR R & R

SETTING UP A NIGHT DEFENSIVE POSITION (NDP)

HEADING TO HONG KONG FOR R & R

FAMOUS FLOATING RESTAURANT AT HONG KONG

MY TAXI RIDE TO LUNCH AT FLOATING RESTAURANT

ORAWON — MY DINNER DATE AT PRESIDENTIAL
HOTEL IN HONG KONG

11. Incoming

TEMPORARY BASE CAMPS

What had happened during the first few months of in-country, I will never forget. We were getting used to the routine of climbing on choppers every few days and using the element of surprise when making contact with the enemy. This particular mission was to be about two to three weeks in length. We felt it in our hearts that this was going to be something big. We knew this because of the size of the operation. We left Tay Ninh Base Camp early in the morning on groups of twelve slicks. All our weapons were loaded and at the ready. That somber gut-wrenching feeling took over as we observed the other slicks flying alongside in a staggered formation. Was this to be my last day on earth? When we were dropped off at the LZ (landing zone), we immediately ran to set up a perimeter around the cleared area, which was the size of two football fields. This was S.O.P. (standard operating procedure). If it was a "hot" LZ with the enemy firing at us, we had to counter to quell the attack. This field accommodated our entire battalion of the 3rd of the 21st infantry. We knew we would be at this location for a while when we noticed a lot of colored smoke grenades going off in the infield. These indicated positions for supplies to be dropped by parachute by C-130's. Many supplies, ammunition, and even water-tank trailers were delivered into the LZ. We were then given empty sandbags and instructed to set up defensive positions. While we were building our positions, we heard the engineers blasting away the remaining trees in the LZ with C4 blasting putty. C4 was like soft clay, it was an amazing material. All you had to do was shape it where you wanted to blast, stick in a blasting cap, form the putty around it nice and tight, and wire it to an activating device for an electrical charge. You would then clear yourself out of the way and detonate the actuator and kaboom! The engineers would just place a ring of C4 around the base of a tree, and one blast would take it away. When it came to chowing down our C-rations, we would use a pinch of C4 under a can of beans and franks, or other main dish, and light the marble sized piece and watch it burn like gunpowder to heat up our meal instantly. We all carried a pound in our "ditty" bags.

NECESSARY INJURIES?

We never got used to being pushed off the Huey's ten to fifteen feet above the ground or rice paddies. We were told this had to be done because the turbulence from the propellers would suck up water or dirt and cause harm to the choppers. We had combat gear with us that amounted to thirty-five to seventy pounds on our backs. I remember when my knees crunched into my chest and felt pain in my lower back. I know that helped contribute to the crushed disc I had removed from my fifth lumbar on May 21st, 1985 at the West Haven VA Hospital. I always had pain in my lower back since leaving the service, but it progressively got worse until the pain became unbearable. The operation alleviated most of the pain, but I remain with chronic pain that will never go away. When the Yale interns performed the surgery, they told me that it was the largest disc they had ever removed. They also informed me that it resembled a fried egg crushed between my vertebrae and they had to use nipper pliers to remove all the pieces. In the thirty-five years since the surgery, it has been a daily struggle to not give in to the gnawing pain.

UNNECESSARY INJURIES

The secured area was large enough for about six slicks to land and take-off in succession. The heat and humidity were unbearable, even for the slicks. Word got around through the grapevine, that some officers were parachuting into this LZ, so they could earn their "wings" (jump wing badges) for parachuting during war-time. They jumped out of C-130 cargo planes. It all backfired on them as some broke their legs and sprained their ankles because the altitude just wasn't enough to open their chutes properly. Hate to say it, but it was an on-going joke between the troops for a while. Another thing that happened at this LZ was with the slicks and the affect that the heat and humidity had on them. The slicks were lined up one day to transport a platoon of us to a new area of operation. We would usually load six to eight of us, a squad size, with gear on each slick. It happened to be just past noon on this particular mission and well over 100 degrees. I didn't see it, but we heard that one of the choppers had a tough time gaining altitude and hooked it's landing frame on some tree limbs and somersaulted over. Some of the troops were injured, resulting in broken legs, arms, and serious bruising. From then on, the chopper crews had us lessen the loads accordingly. The weight, heat, and humidity were a factor that had a bearing on the engine's performance. While all this action was taking place, our positions were ready by the end of the day.

NIGHT DEFENSIVE POSITION

We built a wall of sandbags about twelve feet long and three feet tall in front of our position adjacent to a tree, which was about eight inches in diameter. It was enough to protect us substantially from incoming fire, mortars, and such from outside the perimeter. We dug a trench behind this wall, which provided the dirt to fill the sandbags and provide us with further protection. We were positioned in three-man teams, so through the night, one soldier would be on watch rotating his time with his comrades. One hour on, two hours, hopefully, of sleep. We placed our three claymore mines ten-fifteen meters out in front of our position, spaced apart accordingly. The activators were set just behind our wall, so we would know exactly where they were. We made sure our weapons were at the ready. We also took a mental note of where our gear, water, and ammo were, so we would be able to find them in the dark. The nights were mostly pitch-black in the Nam, especially in the jungle. I never approved of anyone smoking in my position, let alone in any position, while out in the boonies. I just didn't get it. It gave your location away. We were notified at dusk where the listening posts and ambushes would be located. Friendly-fire was always a danger to be reckoned with. There were 8,000 incidents of friendly-fire statistics during the Vietnam War. On the first night in this position, my watch included midnight to one o'clock. I was woken up abruptly at midnight and positioned my head with steel-pot attached against the tree while sitting on the sandbag wall. It was always amazing to me just how quickly you would fall asleep after your watch was up. As soon as you laid down, you were asleep. Another thing, do not go to sleep during your watch! Charlie just might sneak up on your position and slit your throats, it had been done. If we caught anyone sleeping on their watch, we would kick them in the head, helmet or no helmet. While on watch, everything goes through your mind, and I mean everything. Thoughts of home, thoughts of the day's events, and always the thought of, *Am I going to make it?* It was dead silent as I was peering out into the pitch-black darkness. I kept on blinking, not only to stay awake but to erase the false images that I was beginning to think were real. I was just checking my wristwatch and was just about ready to wake up the next sentry. It was 1 A.M. I was still leaning against the tree when all of a sudden, I was thrown off, blasted back through the air, landing on my head, which was still in my helmet, with amazing force. Flares from the LZ suddenly lit up the whole sky. We didn't know what happened or what it was. There was no incoming fire. It became so quiet, we figured it wasn't caused by the enemy. We settled back into the night routine. A warrant officer showed up within fifteen minutes of the explosion. I explained to him that I was thrown off my roost next to the tree. Using his flashlight, he checked around our position and the front of the tree. He dug out a piece of steel that weighed about a pound right next to where my head was resting. It took him all of ten minutes to dig the fragment out. He also explained to us that a soldier from another platoon was sitting on top of his bunker roof and got a piece of the same round lodged in his butt. He was medevac'd out immediately to a base hospital. His position was about 200 meters behind ours. Later in the morning, when the sun came up, two warrant officers came by to check the tree again and the front of our position. They informed us that the "explosion" was friendly-fire. The round happened to hit a large tree fifty to one-hundred meters to our front. We began to think, *Where would it have landed if it didn't hit that tree?* It was from a "155" Howitzer round fired from Cu-Chi, Vietnam, twenty-five miles away, the headquarters of the 25th Infantry Division. It was meant to hit our area as VC were expected to be in this area. This was common practice. Evidently they didn't realize we were operating out of this area at that time. Gladly we didn't hear from them during our stay. They just so happened to be our main fire support base when we needed them, so they remained on alert.

NDP WHERE FRIENDLY FIRE HIT

Newly cleared LZ with re-supply

Buddies along-side heading to LZ

Author on left w/ M-60 at NDP

MORE RE-SUPPLY

MORE SEARCH AND DESTROY MISSIONS

12. First Injury

The first week of December 1966, I was a member of a platoon size patrol, another search and destroy mission, not far from our base camp. It was the beginning of our fifth month pounding the boonies and wondering if we will ever return to the world. It was always on your mind. We constantly checked if our weapon was at the ready, if our thumb was on the safety, and if your closest buddy was paying attention to doing the best he could if the shit hit the fan. By this time, I gave up wearing socks. The ones that rotted on my feet, I threw away and never bothered to wear any more. They were always soaking wet and were just too much trouble to worry about. I placed white nylon screened inserts in the inside of my jungle boots for a little cushioning and lived with it. "Hey," if the VC could get along wearing sandals in the jungle, I could go sock-less. As we trudged along in this steam-bath, filthy-dirty, only worrying if our rifle or machine-gun was clean, I was suddenly surprised by a flying tree branch. Was it a "booby-trap?" I never found out. It hit me in the face, injuring mostly my left eye socket. I was treated on the spot by our medic and sent back to base camp by medevac that evening. Back at base camp, I was treated again and was found that I needed further care.

SAIGON

Preparations were made for me to be transported to Tan San Nhut air field in Saigon and further transported to down-town Saigon to have an appointment with an eighty-two-year-old Vietnamese woman eye surgeon. I was instructed to wear civilian clothes while on my journey. This was mandatory and a pre-cautionary measure, so I wouldn't be noticed as a soldier and an easy target. No one knew how many North Vietnam soldiers or VC were in and around downtown Saigon at the time. I was patched up with a black eye patch, the light bothered my eye so much. The trip to Saigon was quite an experience. All I had with me was my paper-work, a map of where I would eat, an address of the surgeon's office, and fortunately my old 1949 c. Brownie Hawkeye cam-era. That crude camera proved to be worth its weight in gold, for I have the most wonderful photo collection of my time spent in Vietnam. When I arrived in downtown Saigon, I felt like a tourist on a world tour. The city was bustling as though there wasn't even a war going on. Using the best of my ability with the Vietnamese phrases I learned, I hob-knobbed through the city on a rick-shaw and made it to the officer's mess hall at the U.S. embassy. There were military police guarding the entrance, as well as sand-bag bunkers set up. I presented my orders and was let in promptly. I was shocked when I noticed the accommodations the officers had while eating my first meal there. The provisions were better than I had experienced in my whole military career thus far. The hall was air conditioned, and there were young Vietnamese waitresses, dressed in white traditional ao dai dresses, taking the orders and serving the food. One seventeen-year-old waitress caught my eye. Her name was Lin. She seemed to be overly friendly toward me, and I became overwhelmed. Of course I had been spending months in the jungle, so maybe it was my mind playing tricks on me. I did the best I could carrying on a conversation with her and told her I would be returning for dinner that evening. I went out on the city to take in the culture and the sites it had to offer. I was surprised at what the street vendors had in their display cases. Many had American products for sale, such as cigarettes, chewing gum, and many other trinkets. I guess this is what was called the "black market." I was never the bar type or much of a drinker, so I never entered a bar while there. I took a few more photos while roaming the main thoroughfare. After touring the city that afternoon, I returned to the mess hall for dinner. I learned then where my sleeping quarters would be. They were right in the embassy building. I hit the sack early that evening, so I would have a fresh start in the morning to travel to my eye appointment. It was the first time in four months that I slept on a mattress, and my, it felt great. After a great breakfast, I was on my way to my appointment, which wasn't too far from downtown. When I was finally treated by the surgeon, I was told the only care she would recommend was to keep the eye socket lubricated with the medication she provided and for me to wear the eye patch until my eye healed. I left the office and walked back to the mess hall for lunch. I was getting used to the great meals I was having here and not eating out of green metal cans. Back at the embassy, I noticed Lin was working again.

I got her attention when I remarked, "Co-dep-wah," which meant "Hello, pretty girl." It caught her by surprise, so we began to strike up a conversation the best we could. I spoke the phrases I knew. I guess I did fairly well because she requested that I join her for a movie that evening. I accepted and met her in front of the embassy building after dinner that evening. I thought to myself that this would be a good opportunity to learn more about this country's culture. We met on time and walked a couple blocks to the theater. We entered the movie theater, and I was suddenly taken aback. Here I was, a tall, white, American male clothed in western garb and having a patch on my eye. I was accompanying an attractive, young, Vietnamese girl. All eyes in the theater seemed to focus on us. Things settled down when we seated ourselves and the film began to project. The theater was full, which surprised me with this war going on, and I soon calmed down while my blushing subsided. It was very difficult to absorb the entertainment qualities of the film. The speech was in French, and half the projection on the screen was captioned with Vietnamese, Chinese, English, and another language that I wasn't familiar with. You could barely make out the film. I was so glad I attended the movie; it was a great learning experience. I told Lin, in the best dialog I could muster, that I would be returning to my unit at Tay Ninh in the morning and that I would see her at breakfast. It was sad to part ways with Lin at breakfast, I must admit. We exchanged addresses, but I lost hope that I would ever hear from her again. A few days later, while back in the boonies, I received a heartwarming letter from Lin that cheered up my day. I returned a note to her but sadly never heard from her ever again. I hopped on a shuttle after breakfast that took me to Tan-San Nhut air base. I then hooked up with a daily run on a C-130 that took me to my base camp at Tay Ninh. While on the flight back to my unit, I thought about the life style of what was going on in the city of Saigon that I experienced. I felt a deep sadness for what my buddies were going through in the field. The officers, MP's, and REMF were living the "life of Riley" on a vacation it seemed while serving out their military commitment. The concept just didn't seem fair, but I realize it was the luck of the draw. The grunts were at the bottom of the totem-pole. I arrived late morning back at my platoon. It was too quiet; something didn't seem right. I changed into my jungle fatigues and checked out my weapons and gear. I was then told that on the previous ambush patrol my platoon was on, two of my dear friends were killed and two others badly wounded. The depressing mood in camp didn't go away for days, and it still lingers in my thoughts. Whenever I visit the Vietnam Wall in Washington, D.C., I place my hand over December 12th, 1966 and the names of James R. Van Cedarfield and Anthony Schiavalino. They will always be remembered. Losing our first "brothers," those we trained with from the beginning at Fort Devens, had a lasting effect on all of us. We became more conscious, suspicious, and realized, to a greater degree, of the reality of war, how horrible it was, and what it could bring. Grab-ass was down to a minimum as we buckled down to make sure we performed our duties to a higher perspective. What happened in the past week was a wake-up call that let us know that some of us wouldn't be going home alive.

MILITARY POLICE CHECKING BARS

I RODE A RICKSHAW TO GET AROUND

FAMOUS WAR STATUE IN SAIGON

Black market vendor in down-town Saigon

Saigon taxis

S. Vietnamese soldier (ARVN) with loaded Thompson Sub M.G.

Camera I kept in canteen pouch throughout my tour

AUTHOR AT NEW JERSEY "WALL"

13. The Aborted Mission

"Courage Is Being Scared to Death but Saddling up Anyway"

John Wayne

Our battalion was set up at a temporary base camp for a couple weeks far from Tay Ninh. A planned company sized search and destroy mission left the LZ at 1 P.M. Most patrols left early in the morning to beat the excruciating heat of the day. If the patrol took you through the jungle, it would help by providing shade from the sun. The shade also harnessed the cooler night air that was left over from the evening, if ninety plus degrees is considered cool. This particular day, we set out directly across a large rice paddy in the glaring sun. We were keeping our distance between one another in the usual five to ten meters covering the size of a few football fields. The lead command was toward the front of the left front flank. My machine gun team was situated toward the center of the right flank. Only about twenty minutes into the mission, a medevac chopper arrived to extricate a soldier overcome by heat exhaustion. A fellow soldier shouted out that his thermometer read 130 degrees. The reflection off the water that beamed into our faces and bodies was like steam and became unbearable. After about five or six episodes of medevac extractions, the gung-ho commanding officer decided to call off the mission and send the company back to the LZ. We found out later that heat cramps were affecting him, and he finally realized that it was a mistake to patrol at that time of day. What was he trying to prove, putting his men in jeopardy like that?

FACING CHARLIE

The following morning, we headed out early and took a different route. We figured Charlie would've been waiting for us on the other side of the same rice paddy and could have wiped us out. At least the command used a little common sense this time out. By late morning we found ourselves deep into VC territory. As we slowly moved along, we began to notice telltale signs of human presence. There were broken branches and twigs here and there, and then the strange smell of smoke permeated all around us. The triple jungle canopy overhead gave the enemy great cover so they couldn't be spotted from the air. The trails that we were finding were freshly matted down by considerable traffic. All of a sudden, a loud explosion broke the silence that we were trying to retain. We were immediately notified that a booby-trap had just gone off on the left flank. We had just walked into a deserted VC base camp. We were ordered not to touch anything, stay as motionless as possible, and back out exactly the way we came in. Word spread rapidly that Bob Dozer, a squad leader from the first platoon had taken the full force of a tree-hung booby-trap through the side of his face. We cautiously continued on searching for Charlie. We set up a perimeter around a clearing and Sgt. Dozer was medevac'd back to a hospital. Sad to say, the injuries he received changed his life forever. Too bad for them if they had returned there when we left. We felt the earth tremble when those five-hundred pounders were dropped. Nothing could survive those direct hits. Another day we were blessed that Charlie didn't want to face us during daylight hours.

THE BLESSED AIR FORCE

Another search and destroy mission, they never seemed to end. This day we found ourselves close to the Ho-Chi-Minh trail. Our "B" company was ordered to move rapidly in the direction where a large contingent of VC were spotted by a propeller powered spotter plane. As we moved along, that sickening feeling in our stomachs returned, almost like being punched in the gut. The feeling always had a resurgence when there was a good chance we would be facing the enemy in battle, going on an ambush, or just knowing you would soon be in harm's way. We moved along on well-worn paths, our weapons at the ready. We were preparing to go into a meat grinder. We noticed large craters all over the area. This was not virgin war-zone territory. All of a sudden, we were halted while our platoon leader answered a call on the PRC-25. We were notified to remain at this location while F-4 Phantoms were being called in to pummel the spotted VC. We set-up two-man positions and gazed at the distance about a mile away. The tiny spotter plane was doing loops over the intended targets. Then without warning, out of the clouds shot F-4 jets firing their rockets and dropping their bombs. What a wonderful site. After about thirty minutes, we were ordered to return to the previous night's camp to await further orders. We loved the Air Force!

NVA SLEEPING COT

NVA Bicycles

Trudging through rice paddy

SEARCH AND DESTROY

14. My Turn to Die

RANK HAS ITS PRIVILEGES

Another company search and destroy mission was to take place. This time we were to sweep directly through a dense jungle. No trails, no paths, just spread out in columns obeying the rules of jungle warfare and chop through the foliage keeping the distance between one another. Elements of the 25th Infantry Division were in a blocking formation far beyond our path of direction. Through surveillance and intelligence, it was known the enemy was in the area. Approximately a regiment sized VC encampment was expected to be lurking in these surroundings, upwards of up to 2,500 NVA soldiers. Being in Nam for about five months now, the search and destroy missions were becoming routine. Not so routine to let our guard down. We learned the fact that we had to look out for your buddy's asses, as they were looking out for yours. We became a tighter knit group than ever and became very good at what we had to accomplish. We were performing the tasks at hand in order to bring each other home alive. Individually we became extremely cautious. Caches of rice and weapons were being found everywhere. Even piles of discarded bicycles were just left unattended. We stopped for a ten- minute break while the platoon leaders communicated with headquarters to see what further direction we would be taking. Those of us who wished downed some C-rations and water to keep their energy levels up and to keep from getting dehydrated. We looked around to one another as we noticed everyone's mood was worsening. We knew all hell was about to break loose. Master Sgt. James Durfee, my platoon Sgt from day one, abruptly handed me a machete and commanded me to be on point on the right flank of this sweep when we continued on. Besides, being a tunnel-rat or being on an ambush patrol, the duty of being on "point" was the most feared and hated duty in Nam. I personally believe it is the worst duty. Through all my training, Sgt. Durfee and I never saw eye to eye. He despised me. Being such a "strack" soldier, it was strange that he had two downfalls. One being that he was a physical failure. He couldn't perform one push-up. His nickname throughout our training regime was "spoon-chest." The other downfall was that he actually couldn't measure up to the pressures of combat. Everything he taught us, he personally couldn't handle. When this day's events subsided, it was claimed that Sgt. Durfee suffered a nervous breakdown and was sent back to the states. I beg to differ. He held back my promotions and medals a few times as he just had it in for me. I was the physical specimen that he wasn't. All through basic training, we just didn't hit it off. I would mention his chain smoking as being unhealthy, and he would counter with more push-ups or more K.P. (kitchen police duty). He was self-conscious that his derogatory nickname came from me. I therefore became his" whipping-boy." So on this company mission, Sgt. Durfee thought that he would have his day. I took the machete from him and gave him a stare that would remain with him for the rest of his life. My buddies questioned him as to why he was putting me on point when I was the machine gunner. He just shut them up. I left my M-60 with my crew and grabbed an M-16. I began to cut through the thick jungle undergrowth with aplomb. I can't believe to tell you the feelings that were going through my mind. They were not good. We were spread out in two flanks with individual scouts ten meters out parallel to the flanks. I was at least ten meters ahead of the nearest soldier swinging the machete with my right hand while holding on to my M-16 at the ready in my left hand. I was witnessing common jungle noises as I trudged ahead. Moving through the jungle in the intense heat and humidity for over an hour, I occasionally glanced back to see my buddy signaling to proceed. Wiping the perspiration constantly and slapping the bugs and mosquitoes didn't help the task at hand. Eventually I entered a small clearing. I began to notice a dead silence, an aura that you can only imagine that takes place while viewing a horror film. Most of the trees were stripped of foliage. I was entering a VC base camp. All of a sudden, in a split second of time, a loud shot, a thud, and popping of bullets began to whiz around me. An RPG round hit a tree only five feet to my left and fell next to my left boot. It hit the tree at an angle without detonating the firing pin at the nose or didn't have enough distance to arm itself, only being about thirty feet from being fired when it hit the tree. I immediately dove to the base of an ant hill, which was directly to the right front of me. I never got the chance to return fire. The two VC that were left behind in a bunker to guard their camp while their unit was on a mission, took off running down a trail behind them. Lucky for me they took off, and unlucky for them, they ran into a unit of the 25th Infantry Division who cut them to pieces with an M-60 machine gun. It turned out that this was one of the closest near-death experiences of my tour. It has always been on my mind that if they just used their rifle to shoot me in the chest, I wouldn't be here today. Soon after, when my platoon mustered together, I searched for Sgt. Durfee. That is when I was told he was sent back to headquarters. I never saw him again.

FOUND MORE NVA/VC RICE

NVA BUNKER FROM WHERE I WAS SHOT AT

NVA LATRINE

15. Rotation to the 4th Infantry Division

After spending seven months in Nam, it became obvious that the 196th Light Infantry Brigade couldn't go on with the same members for the entire one year at the same base camp. The unit couldn't just pick up and return to the states, the base camp would be empty. During the end of operation Gadsden and the beginning of operation Junction City, command decided to deploy a percentage of the troops of the 196th to other units in Nam. This way they would get to finish their tours as short-timers in their "new" unit. All that were scheduled to be transferred had the hope of joining a non-combat unit, such as an MP company or a rear-echelon security group. Hoping and praying didn't help one bit. I was not so lucky. My MOS meant that I would remain in a rifle platoon for the remainder of my tour. I received my orders the first week of March '67 to be relocated to the 3rd brigade of the 4th Infantry Division, 2nd battalion, 12th Infantry, "C" company. Their headquarters were located twelve miles east of Tay Ninh at Dau Tieng in the Michelin Rubber Plantation. Those transferred along with me, including myself, were not happy campers. Through the grapevine we heard of horrifying details of encounters the 4th had with 272nd and 273rd regiments of the 9th NVA Division. I left Tay Ninh base camp, and most of my 196th brothers, the first week of March. We traveled in a convoy of "deuce and a half's" accompanied by our military records, combat gear, duffel bags, and any other personal items that we wished to take along. At about the same time frame, the 196th headed north to Chu Lai and eventually became an element of the Americal Division. The 25th Infantry Division, Tropic Lightning, would take command of the Tay Ninh base camp.

While on the convoy to become a replacement in the 4th Infantry division, I witnessed a few unscrupulous events. The first, while on the twelve-mile jaunt, was when the soldiers from the transportation unit handling our relocation, thought it was their right to trade off cases of C-rations to the local villagers who were shadowing us in return for pot, cigarettes, trinkets, and other black-market paraphernalia. The other misconduct that took place happened when a couple of transferred soldiers suggested we open our military records and remove any records pertaining to punishment, such as an article fifteen or any records of having an R and R. They were hoping they would get to go on a second R and R when joining their new unit. Surprisingly this was an odd way to transport the personal military records of these combat soldiers. When I arrived at the base camp of "C" company, 2nd of the 12th, I carried my gear to the First Sergeant's command tent. I presented the First Sergeant my orders. He informed me that the company was out on a mission and which tent and cot I would be occupying. I had an onrush of bad vibes when I later found out that I was replacing a soldier that was killed in battle. We were situated among thousands of rubber trees on the edge of the Michelin Rubber plantation, only a couple hundred feet from our main gate to the city of Dau Tieng and adjacent to the 4th's helipad and airstrip. That night another replacement and myself noticed the base camp was still vacated. We proceeded to investigate the surroundings around a massive above-ground swimming pool that was located right in our company premises. The temperature being in the nineties, we proceeded to get into our bathing suits and climb the stairs alongside the pool. We dove in and had an enjoyable swim. Before we knew it, we were reprimanded for being there and were told the pool was off limits. We were scurried away to our tents and were never allowed to use the pool again. The following morning, my "new" company returned from their mission. I fit in quite comfortably when I answered many questions about my previous service while I was making all new friends. We were all in the same boat, as it were.

NOTHING CHANGED

My wishes were not granted. I remained a killing machine that I was trained to be. We were now deep into operation Junction City, the largest operation of the war to date. Interesting to note, at this time, Operation Attleboro, which was initiated by the 196th, took place from September 14th to November 24th, 1966 with a result of VC/NVA casualties: 2,278 killed, thirty-four prisoners, U.S. casualties: 282 killed; 1,576 wounded. Operation Junction city, while deploying twenty-two U.S. battalions, took place from February 22nd to May 14th, 1967 with a result of VC/NVA casualties: 2,130 killed, forty-four prisoners, U.S. casualties: 155 killed, 494 wounded. All this took place while fighting the same NVA 9th division/272-273rd regiments who were based in Cambodia. One major battle stands out in my mind that my unit was involved in. It was the battle of LZ Gold, or also named the "Battle of Suoi Tre," which took place on March 21st, 1967. During the battle at the fire support base, in early morning while entering from the southwest, my platoon was ordered to quell our movement and lay as close to the ground as possible. Units of the 2/22nd Infantry Mechanized, in their M113 APC's and the 2nd bat. 34th Armor Reg. in their M48A3 tanks were charging right by us heading toward the center of the battle, firing everything they had because the LZ was being over-run. If it wasn't for the Armor or the Cavalry, the outcome of the battle would have surely been different. NVA casualties: 647 killed, seven captured, U.S. casualties: thirty-six killed, 190 wounded. I was able to take a few photos while being pinned down and while leaving the battle zone by choppers. A very sad occurrence happened on that day. A good friend of mine, Jim Brewer, who was one of the originals from the 196th and who was also transferred to the 2/12th, succumbed to a direct mortar round while defending the fire base that day. Rest in eternal peace, my brother.

For the next three and a half months, I lived in the jungle 90 percent of the time chasing Charlie. We didn't change our clothes, we ate out of cans unless a hot meal was choppered out to us if it was deemed safe, which wasn't often. It puzzled us as to what the slime they were spraying overhead and was landing just about everywhere we ended up. Our main concern was to keep our weapons clean and at the ready and to make sure our buddies were always at the ready.

BANGKOK

A pleasant surprise came one afternoon when a hot meal was flown out to us. I was granted an R & R and was headed to Bangkok for four days. I was allowed to fly back that evening with the returning meal-run. I instantly became a happy camper. A day later, I was flying out of Tan Son Nhut air base wearing my dress uniform. I brought along civies to wear, so my dress uniform would stay clean and presentable. All the guys on this R & R were talking about the famous massage parlors of Bangkok that they heard about from their buddies that had gone there previously. This sparked an interest, so I tagged along with a couple of grunts I met on the flight over. After we changed into our civies at our hotel, the three of us chipped in for a cab and headed right over to one of the establishments to see if the legends were true. We were driven up to a modern one-story brick building about the size of a bank. The large picture windows, which adorned the front, were deeply tinted so you couldn't see in. As we entered, we were met with a site for sore eyes. There was a party atmosphere going on with the latest of popular music permeating the air. Beautiful young Asian ladies dressed in white uniforms were parading around, making sure your time spent there was to your liking. We settled down in one of the sofas and purchased a drink, so we could learn what the routine was here. The ladies immediately made us comfortable and explained that if one of them sparked an interest, you could choose her by the number she was wearing on her chest. You would then pay the $3 fee and be escorted by her to one of the many booths in the back of the building for a Turkish bath and massage. There was also a large one-way mirror in this lounge, so you could observe the ladies in their own private lounge when they didn't realize they were being looked upon. I gazed with wide eyes through this mirror and eventually chose #9. She came out and sat with me on the sofa and began to converse as though she was my long-lost friend. She made me feel so at ease. After a while, she suggested that it was time for my bath. I joined her for the rest of the hour that I had left in the bath and massage booth. I had such a pleasant time there that I came back the next day and chose #9 again. We skipped all formalities and spent the full hour in the booth. It was the best bath that I ever had. That afternoon I decided to see some of the country, figuring I would never get the chance to return. I went on a "Temple Tour" and added to my photo collection of my time spent serving in the military. I have some great photos of Buddhas, Temples, Monks, and the landscape of Bangkok. It was very hard to return to the life of a combat soldier after R & R. We had to do what we had to do.

MY NEW UNIT — 4TH INFANTRY DIVISION

SHOWERS AT 2ND BAT./12TH INF. 4TH INFANTRY DIVISION AT DAU TIENG

"C" COMPANY 2/12 FROM MY "HOOTCH"

MY TWO NEW BUDDIES FROM CHICAGO

Convoy to the "4th" - illegal trading with GI's

More village patrolling

NEW "HOOTCHES" BEING BUILT

M113 ARMOURED CAVALRY ASSAULT VEHICLE
(APC) — FIRING 50 CAL. GOING BY AUTHOR

Battle with Huey and APCs involved

Leaving battle in chopper

Tanks and APCs in perimeter

AUTHOR AT POOL FIRST NIGHT WITH 2/12 4TH INFANTRY DIVISION

AUTHOR ON RIGHT WITH "C" CO. 3RD PLATOON
MY NEW ASSIGNMENT

Bangkok temples

The famous "Wat Pho" reclining Buddha

16. Short & Home to Civilian Life

GETTING SHORT

As time went on, my feelings of making it home grew every day. I wrote on my helmet cover each day the number of days left of my tour. Being a short timer had its benefits. I became very good friends with my new platoon leader of "C" company 2/12th. During idle chat, he questioned me why I hadn't received my promotion to specialist 4th class. I told him the whole story about my platoon sergeant's rift against me all through training and my in-country service and how he tried to get me killed by putting me on point. The lieutenant found my orders, and my promotion was submitted within the next few days. He also told me that when I had thirty days left in my tour, he would pull me out of the front lines and have me guard the main gate during the daylight hours. This was a godsend. I thought I had been blessed and felt I had a much better chance of making it home. He also gave me a mission to perform. I would accompany a squad leader from another platoon to deliver a packet to headquarters in Saigon. Sgt. Davis, also a transfer from the 196th, and I left the following morning from the Dau Tieng air strip on the daily shuttle to Tan Son Nhut. Sgt. Davis had a rebellious nature about him, so I knew I had to be cautious at what he suggested we do while spending our day in downtown Saigon. We brought a small ruck-sack with us with the necessary toiletries and a change of civies. When we arrived at the air base, we found an Army shuttle that was heading into downtown. We dropped off the package to headquarters and proceeded to enjoy the sights and sounds of the capital of south Vietnam. I told Sgt. Davis about my previous time when I was injured, and we could get a great meal at the officers' mess. Being the rebel that he was, Sgt. Davis was all for it, so we proceeded to the officers' mess hall for our lunch. The classified orders that accompanied us was the ticket that easily got us through the heavily guarded door. Sgt. Davis was also taken aback, as I was, when he experienced the difference the REMF's had as compared to the grunt's life in the field. After the hearty lunch, we decided to tour the city and find a hotel to stay in close by, so we would be ready to take the morning shuttle back to Tan Son Nhut and then to our base camp. On the way to finding our room for the night, we discovered the PX nearby. We had our monthly allotment cards with us and used them to purchase a case of 7-UP. We didn't know it, but the civilians were crazy for it. When we found a small hotel, more like a run-down boarding house, we paid for our room with the case of 7-UP. My skills with the Vietnam language paid off. Our room cost us under $2. The following morning, I was ready to seek out the shuttle that would take us to Tan Son Nhut. Sgt. Davis wouldn't have any part of it. He wanted to spend an extra day and night on the town. He said he would take full responsibility and explain to the higher ups, that we missed our transportation. Since I was traveling with him, I went along. I should have used my better judgement. We toured the city for the day and ventured into the Cholon section, which was the Chinese district of Saigon. Before we knew it, night time was getting near, so we had to search out another place to stay. We decided to use the same plan as the night before. We bought another case of 7-UP and carried it along with us while scouting for our night's abode. I don't know what got into us, but we rode on a rickshaw deep into the suburbs. I used my skills again conversing with the locals in a middle-class neighborhood it seemed. For the price of a case of 7-UP, we got to stay at an elderly woman's home. She stated that it was an honor for us to stay in her own oversized bed. We must have been quite the special guests. She prepared the bedroom for us and let us be. There was even a large paddle fan in the ceiling directly over us creating a pleasant breeze. We used her simple facilities to wash up and shave. Can you imagine, the thought of our throats being slit that night only slightly came to mind. The following morning, we woke up late. We bid a friendly good-bye and were on our way. We made it to the officers' mess for a wonderful breakfast. We missed the shuttle, so Sgt. Davis decided to spend the day in downtown Saigon and visit the bars at night. I tried to change his mind, but he wouldn't listen. We didn't realize there was a curfew at 11 P.M. in Saigon for the military. We were abruptly picked up in a bar by the MPs and held overnight. The following morning, we were shuttled to Tan Son Nhut and flown back to our unit in Dau Tieng. Wouldn't you know it? A couple days later, a report came down to our headquarters that I disobeyed curfew. I was issued an article 15, a misdemeanor charge, a minor infraction on my military record. Back out in the field I went. The daily grind of search and destroy missions, ambush patrols, helicopter assaults, avoiding snakes, insects, animals, and the worst thing of all, getting killed, was the life of the infantryman.

MY LAST THIRTY DAYS

It was one of the happiest days of my life when I had thirty days left of my tour. My platoon leader didn't go back on his word. I was sent to guard the main gate in a bunker for eight hours a day during day-time. It was just like having a normal job. No more ambushes, search and destroy missions, and living like a groundhog. I took daily showers, was issued a clean set of fatigues, ate at the mess hall, and felt like a human being again. I watched the daily life of downtown Dau Tieng right from my own bunker. I was only about fifty yards from my company camp ground. On the walk to the bunker and back, I passed the company laundry drop, a little bamboo hut manned by two young Vietnamese girls. It was called Annie's Laundry. An elderly Papa-son (a Vietnamese gentleman) picked up the laundry daily and of course returned the so-called clean laundry from the day before. When we were in the field, we never had this luxury. Hell, I never wore socks or underwear. While I was occupying my bunker at the main gate, I would notice one of the pretty laundry girls as I passed every day. You couldn't miss it; her belly was growing. She had a boyfriend that was in our unit, a nice kid that would hang around the laundry hut. We used to see her sitting on his lap all the time. You don't have to be a rocket scientist to figure out how she swallowed the watermelon seed. An estimated 50,000 Vietnamese children were fathered by American servicemen during the Vietnam war. These "Amerasian" children were considered legally Americans and most became social outcasts in Vietnam.

The duty at the main gate was great. I had plenty of time to think. I was still doing hundreds of push-ups daily. I thought of my past eleven months in the bush. The close calls to death and why I had made it thus far and others hadn't was always on my mind. I was so glad I brought that old Brownie camera with me and sent the rolls home to my mom to be developed. I was still taking photos at the main gate, the laundry hut, my squad, and the young Vietnamese girls that would come on post to work the rubber trees. Every day I thought about what I would do to my best friend and my wife who deceived me. It was such a let-down. On August 3rd, my platoon leader and good friend brought over a wooden crate that was assigned to me to be filled with my personal belongings to be sent home. Grunts were allowed 200 pounds, officers, 300 pounds and up. I stuffed that crate with my old jungle fatigues, jungle boots, helmet, gas mask, entrenching tool, web gear, my two forty-pound dumbbells, a hand grenade, civilian clothes, and other incidentals.

When a warrant officer came by to inspect it, he said, "Oh, Augie, just nail it up." He didn't even look inside. I gave my civilian foot locker that I bought in downtown Tay Ninh, to one of my buddies. I was on my way to embark on the "freedom bird" the next day.

HOME TO CIVILIAN LIFE

August 4th, 1967 couldn't come soon enough. I wished all my buddies best of luck as I left my tent in my dress uniform. I was transported to Tan Son Nhut air base in a C-130. I flew to California on a commercial Jet, then onto McGuire Air Force Base in New Jersey. I spent a couple days at Fort Dix taking mental tests and having physical exams performed on me to see if I was competent to join the civilian life again. I flew from McGuire A.F.B. to Bradley Field in Connecticut where my mom and dad met me on the tarmac. I stepped onto the runway and literally kissed the ground. I had survived. I had this strange feeling while walking through the airport. Here I was, dressed in my military uniform and people were totally ignoring me. They were purposely turning away from me. I wasn't concerned with myself, but my uniform represented my fellow soldiers and what they were going through on the other side of the world. To this day, I have a hard time understanding that. I'll always remember the infamous quote, "All gave some; some gave all." The experiences I witnessed for the twenty-two months of my service during the Vietnam War certainly had a bearing on my life that has lasted me my lifetime, good and bad. I truly feel blessed that I survived. God bless all my military comrades.

ANNIE'S LAUNDRY

MICHELIN RUBBER PLANTATION EMPLOYEES AT OUR CAMPGROUND

ANNIE'S LAUNDRY GIRLS
GIRL IN FRONT SWALLOWED WATERMELON SEED

PIMP - PHOTO TAKEN FROM MAIN GATE

SAIGON - FROM HOTEL WINDOW

CURIOUS GIRL AT MAIN GATE

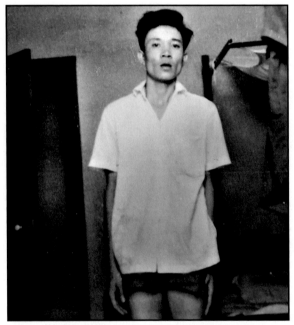

HOTEL ROOM MANAGER WHERE WE STAYED

17. PTSD, Divorces, and Agent Orange

BLENDING BACK INTO CIVILIAN LIFE

I arrived home penniless, save for my release payment from the Army. The monthly combat pay that I sent home to my wife was all spent. The welcome I received from my wife and "Jody" was cold as dry ice. I immediately took up residence with my wife and son at my parent's home. I began to work right away as a roofer's helper with my dad. The 1940 Ford street machine that I left garaged and on blocks was taken apart and left outside by another friend. Even the engine was gone. I was so discouraged, I sold it for a pool table and $250. I contacted my friend, Wayne, who I had met in Nam who now lived in Longmeadow, Massachusetts with his wife, Joanne. I went with them to Holyoke to see the Mr. New England contest, the first body-building contest I ever saw. I was quite impressed. I told Wayne I was training in my mom's basement, so I would compete in the future contests. He had a lot of faith and trust in me. Within a couple weeks, I was able to find an apartment for my family and I in Cromwell, Connecticut, which was only five miles away from my parent's home. I didn't have any plans of making roofing my life-long occupation, so I enrolled in a one-night a week course in computer programming that would take a year to complete and have job placement opportunities. The classroom was fifteen miles away. One rainy night while going to class, I found the class canceled because of the instructor's inability to attend that night.

First Divorce

I turned around and came home early, only to bump into Jody as he was coming out of my apartment. You could tell by the look on his face that he was guilty as sin. It was extremely difficult for me to accept this betrayal. I went in and confronted my wife, who happened to be nude. I had an outburst that caused her to run out of the apartment and pound on an elderly tenant's door. The commotion brought about our eviction, which was quite immediate. I moved back with my parents while my wife and son moved in with hers. We filed for divorce, which I knew was imminent as we barely knew each other, being apart for the fourteen months while I served. The roofing season soon ended, so I had to seek out other employment. I had a commitment to pay weekly support payments to my wife while my divorce was pending, and that was to last a year. The first of February '68, I contacted Pratt & Whitney Aircraft in Middletown to fill out a work application. I was hired on the spot and joined a twelve-week training program to become an engineering draftsman. I was a wiz at trigonometry in high school and was surprised to find out that is what they used exclusively in this business. I completed the program in eight weeks and was moved to the "floor" and joined a friendly group of draftsmen who worked on the JT9D engine, which powered the Boeing "747" jumbo jet. The engine was still in the development stages, so there was plenty of overtime. There were many sixty-hour work weeks to be had. The roofing season started up in March, so I also worked weekends with my dad when he needed me. While all this was taking place, I was able to fulfill the passion I have always had with owning and building a custom street machine. I found a 1960 Corvette nearby that I purchased and began to work on. While all this was going on, I was releasing my frustrations in the gym that I built in my mom's basement. It became an obsession. I was loaded with anxiety and had a short fuse. Word was getting around that I had it "in" for Jody. Before I knew it, and what I was told, Jody became frightened and moved to California, never to be seen in these parts ever again. There was a girl from Old Saybrook, Connecticut that was to begin working on our floor in the file department. From what we heard through the grape-vine, she was pretty attractive and had a jovial nature about her. You had to be eighteen years of age to work at P & W, so she couldn't begin work until April 7th, her eighteenth birthday. When the time Sue arrived (not her real name) and joined the work force, it was obvious that the reports about her were not false. She was a knock-out. During our forty-five-minute lunch breaks, I would eat my brown-bagged lunch at my work station and then saunter outside for some fresh air and usually hang out at the main entrance to our building. Word was getting around (there is always plenty of gossip in work places such as this) that everyone was trying to date Sue. One day I met her in the entrance-way during lunch time and struck up a conversation. We had something in common. She knew my friend John, who initially started me on the weight lifting programs at Hartford Barbell Studio when we were in high school. She liked my '60 Corvette and agreed to go on a date in it on May 10th, a Friday night. Needless to say, on that date, a whirl-wind romance began that lasted for six years. Her mother didn't approve of our dating because I was a Vietnam veteran and had a young son. Sue was her only child and expected her to marry a professional. Sue kept our relationship hidden from her mother, so there wouldn't be any enmity between them. Ten months after meeting Sue, my divorce was finalized. I proved Rose (not her real name) an unfit mother. I was awarded custody of my son. Rose was awarded visitation rights, but as time went on, her showing up dwindled down until she never came around again. Eventually Sue left P & W, so she could pursue a nursing career at the renowned Ona M. Wilcox School of Nursing where she obtained her L.P.N. diploma. We were planning for our future to-gether, so I hired a local builder to begin construction of our dream house. While it was being built, Sue entered the "Miss New London" beauty pageant and won. She then entered the "Miss Middletown" pageant and won. She then went on to win the "Miss Connecticut World" pageant. She then placed sec-ond runner up in the "Miss World-USA pageant, which was partially spon-sored by Bob Hope. While Bob Hope was touring Vietnam with the U.S.O. shows, Sue spent a month with Bob's wife, Dolores, at their California home. It just goes to show how congenial Sue was. Bob paid all expenses. While this was all happening, I continued pumping iron in my basement to relieve frus-trations and improve my physique. In February of 1973, something came over me. I wanted out of spending my time under florescent lights at a board being low man on the totem pole. I enjoyed the physical work more and decided to join my dad for the last year and a half working with him before he retired. I left P & W and went to work full-time roofing. I put my heart and soul into our new home I was having built. I built a full gym in the basement. I installed a shower stall and half bath to complement the gym. I also built a retaining wall myself along the driveway, which was on a slope. I did all the painting and staining in the whole house by working on it at night and weekends. By November of 1973, our house was ready to be moved into. Sue had been pressuring me into marrying her for some time, but I kept putting it off because of the miserable experience I went through with my first marriage. I had cold feet. I was deeply in love with Sue, so I went along with her when she made arrangements with a Justice of the Peace and a doctor to get my blood test. We were married at the Justice of the Peace office in New Britain, Connecticut on November 30th, a Saturday night. Sue brought two friends with her to be witnesses to the ceremony. The four of us celebrated at Jack August seafood restaurant and were pleasantly surprised by the manager that the meal was on them when we told him it was our wedding night. Sue's friends, Holt and Gail, dropped us off at our new home, so we could spend our first night together there. It was a night of bliss until Sue called her mother to tell her the good news.

SECOND DIVORCE

I don't know what her mother's response was, but Sue was so frightened that it caused her to get in her car and return to her parent's house in Old Saybrook. As she was leaving, I told her I would come down in the morning and have a nice family discussion together. I did just that; late Sunday morning, I showed up to something I wish I would never have to witness again in my lifetime. I sat down in the living room and began to explain about the lovely future their daughter and I were about to partake in. Her mother wouldn't have any part of it. She was dressed in black from head to toe. She started to act like a raving maniac, scaring the hell out of her daughter. She got on the floor and spun around like Curley Howard of the Three Stooges, doing the Curley Shuffle. She demanded we get the marriage annulled. It was no use. I couldn't talk with this woman who was out of her mind. I left and returned home. I was heartbroken. Sue hired a local attorney who found a simple solution to our dilemma. He sent me to Port-O-Prince, Haiti for a "quickie" divorce. When I returned from my "all expenses paid trip" to that lovely island, Sue and I carried on our romance with one another for another year, without her mother knowing. I sold the house I had built and moved back into my parent's home. Moving the gym was quite a chore. Thousands of pounds of weights and bolted in equipment had to be moved. I was now living with my parents and my son. The relationship with Sue was slowly dwindling away.

PTSD

All my time was spent training in my basement and focusing on becoming successful. I purchased a brand-new van, which I lettered up myself, and new roofing equipment. I became a work-a-holic! Nothing was getting in my way. I was doing all the hands-on work myself. I was having explosive episodes. I was going through helpers like there was no tomorrow. My helpers were only used as go-fers. I loaded my van at night, so I could be on the job just after dawn in the morning. I worked until dusk most days, then haul myself to the gym to get in a two-hour workout. I estimated all my jobs either on weekends or after work, if I could fit in the time. I did all the secretarial work and accounting. I was a one-man-show. I didn't know it then, but I was a product of Shell Shock, Battle Fatigue, and what's now known as PTSD. And things would get worse.

Agent Orange

I couldn't understand it then, but I was developing epidermal sores all over my body. My son Darin, who had been playing with my jungle fatigues that I sent home, was also experiencing an extreme case of skin disorders. He was further diagnosed with Asperger's Syndrome and has lived with disabilities with symptoms of scoliosis, arthritis, and auto immune issues. He has never worked and is my 100% dependent.

Third Marriage

By the end of 1975, it was over between Sue and I. We had moved on and found ourselves in new relationships. I ended up marrying an army "brat" who was brought up in Korea and Germany. Margaret's (not her real name) father was a full bird colonel, a tank battalion commander, and hero of World War II. I never got to meet him, I wish I had; he had passed away earlier that year. We were married in Margaret's grandmother's home on December 31st, 1975, only after knowing each other for three months. We had two sons together, who I cherished and who Margaret was a helicopter mother to. As a wife, she made the devil look like an angel. I was called a baby killer and other derogatory names right in front of my sons. I never could understand it, I was a good provider and great father. A friend of mine told me that Margaret had a chemical imbalance. I believe it. I tolerated the mental cruelty and became all the more of a work-a-holic and avoided being near that woman as much as I could. I couldn't tolerate being away from my boys if I ever got another divorce. So I stuck it out with the marriage and tried to be the best father I could be. I went through the whole scouting program until both of my boys became Eagle Scouts. I am proud to say I was an assistant Scout Master and thoroughly involved with my boy's success.

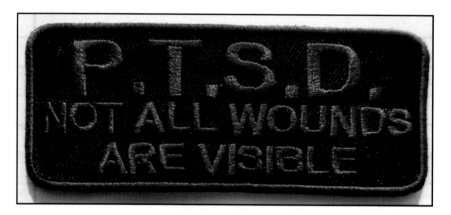

AUTHOR WITH SONS-MARC AND MIKAEL

AUTHOR AT WORK

FIRST STREET ROD I BUILT WHEN I RETURNED HOME-'60 CORVETTE

AUTHOR SHINGLING

Second wife-Sue

Author and Sue

18. Eight Years to Reach the Summit

I am probably repeating myself a little, but I do not want to leave anything out of this story of how I conquered this mission. When I returned from the hell of Vietnam combat, I abruptly removed my dress uniform. We were treated like cow dung as we passed through the airports and train stations on our way home to re-enter the good life that we left behind. It was very difficult to sit still as I became very anxious. I couldn't work enough, and when I wasn't working, I'd be lifting weights. I added on to the weight set that my dad bought me for Christmas when I was seventeen-years-old. I was visiting Forest City Welding when I had some extra money to have benches, racks, and other gym equipment welded up to add on to my home gym in my basement. I couldn't get enough. During 1968 Wayne became more of a mentor. He guided me forward to my first competition, Mr. New England 1968. I was fortunate to place fifth in the tall division. That experience sparked me even further to dedicate myself to winning the Mr. New England title. I was hungry. Every year at Mountain Park in Holyoke, Massachusetts, there were three contests held. These were managed by Mr. Ed Jubinville of Jubinville Gym Equipment, which is still in business. Ed was the world-famous muscle-control artist and judged many of the Mr. Olympia contests, the premier contest in body-building. The Mr. East Coast contest took place at the end of May, the Junior Mr. America at the end of July, and the Mr. New England on Labor Day weekend. In 1969 I began to enter these contests. The East Coast and Junior Mr. America were always tough. Professionals from the big gyms of New York City, Boston, and those that were featured in health magazines would enter. As time wore on, I began to place in those contests. By 1973 and 1974, I placed second in the Mr. New England contest. In 1975 I dedicated myself completely. I studied diet, read diligently about training methods, and focused on the 1975 Mr. New England contest. During this time, steroids and body-building drugs were running rampant. "Juicing" began to become the norm. Juicing was when injectable steroids were used. I would here the term Deca-duroblin would be the way to go when achieving more size and muscularity. It would be injected right into the muscle, usually the thigh or derriere. Before that Dianabol was the tablet to take to achieve more size. Through gym gossip, the muscle-heads would say that the injectables were safer because the "roids" wouldn't pass through your liver and harm you. Luckily I never went "on" any of these as my main reason for training was health. I never smoked, drank, or wouldn't even drink soda. I obeyed the suggestions of Frank Gancarz, who was a power lifter I met at the Hartford Barbell Studio. He drilled it into me to refrain from taking any anabolic steroids and to train naturally was the healthiest way to go. My good friend, Randy Bumgardner, a world record holder in the bench press, mentioned to me that Frank would always mention my name to him that we trained at the Hartford Barbell Studio together. To this day, I am so glad I competed naturally. When Labor Day weekend came, I knew I was ready. I was training two hours a day. I ate many fruits and vegetables. I was eating cans and cans of tuna right out of the can. I was staying away from starches and sugars. It became a science to me. It worked. There were twenty-nine competitors that day. The favorite was a guy named Barry from Boston. He was a monster. He was about 6' 4" and 240 pounds. He and I were chosen from all the other competitors. The pose-down we had lasted about five minutes. What I had over all the other competitors was perfect symmetry. I was declared the winner and was in shock. I finally did it. I climbed this mountain for eight years and reached the summit. This was also the day Charles Gaines and George Butler started filming the documentary-movie *Pumping Iron*. I appear three times in the beginning scenes as this contest was the opening venue for the film. Franco Columbo congratulated me. He was Arnold Schwarzenegger's best friend and training partner and was guest poser that day. Ed Jubinville told me to meet him the next day on Holyoke mountain for a photo shoot. He told me I was in the best shape of my life and to not miss the opportunity to have some great photos taken. I jumped at the chance. Two months later, I entered the Mr. Northeast America contest held at Nashua, New Hampshire. I was elated to win that title also. Joe Weider spoke to me in New York City that winter while I was at the Mr. America contest. He requested that I move to California and go to work under his tutelage. I refused his offer as I had just purchased my father's business the past July and had a family to support. I continued training to a lesser degree while I was putting all my time and effort into my self-employment business.

PHOTOS BY ED JUBINVILLE

HOLYOKE MT. MA- DAY AFTER WINNING

Franco Columbo congratulating me

MR. NEW ENGLAND

1975 AGE 30

AT MR. AMERICA CONTEST-NY CITY

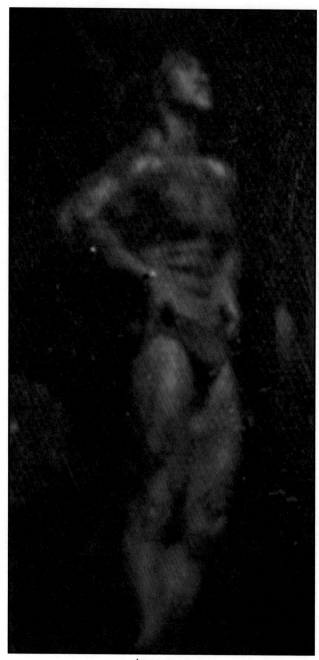

At contest

19. Street-Rodding: A Life-Long Passion

When I was drafted in the summer of 1965, I was enjoying the time of my life. I was working on my hot-rod and attending the weekend, quarter-mile drag races at Connecticut Dragway. My friends and I would pile in my car on Sunday mornings and head to the strip for the day to enjoy our favorite pastime. It hurt so much when I was away for the twenty-two months while I served my country. Those were the times when the best drag racing events took place. When I returned, I bought and built a show-winning 1960 Corvette. By 1970 I was putting most of my time into winning the Mr. New England title, so I sold the Vette to concentrate on that goal. A few years after I achieved my body-building goals, the street-rodding bug hit me again. I was always interested in the "gassers" at the drag races. Those were family cars that were meant to be driven at the speed limit but were now souped up with racing engines. They were fed pump gasoline and not racing fuel, therefore the name gasser originated and stuck. I began to buy and sell gasser style coupes and sedans and stuck to this hobby to this day. I got my son, Marc, interested in the hobby when I told him the story of how I became involved in it. It seemed like ever since Marc could speak, I would convey stories of my dad and I as I was growing up in Middletown, Connecticut. The greatest racing of all time, fifties and sixties drag racing, was included of course!

VETERAN'S GARAGE

In the 1950's, while I was in grammar school and middle school, my dad would always take me on his roof repair rounds on Saturdays. One of these establishments was an old flat-roofed wooden building that had a dirt floor and a fifty-five-gallon oil drum converted into a wood burning stove for heat. It was more like a home-built garage that someone built. When it rained, the water seeped into the floor from the foundation. The building was at 47 Union Street and was called "Veterans Garage" and was owned and managed by Gideon "Joe" Fields, a World War II combat veteran. Joe was most often seen laying on cardboard under old coupes and sedans changing clutches and performing other general repairs. If it was a cold, raw, rainy-day, Joe would be working in mud under the cars while his many so-called friends (drifters and the local riff-raff) would be gathered around the stove telling dirty jokes. I grew up pretty fast in that environment. Joe Fields retired in 1967 and moved to Maine with his wife Elsie. Veterans Garage was leveled when redevelopment came to town. Marc loved the Veterans Garage story, and since I am a Vietnam veteran, we just had to name our hobby garage, "Veteran's Garage". As time went on, Marc and I built some great, award-winning, tribute gassers of the 1960's. We became New England Reps. to Gasser Magazine. I joined Connecticut Street Rod Association, a premiere car club of Connecticut, where I am still a member. I am also a staff writer for Connecticut Cruise News, which has a monthly distribution of 15,000 publications that covers the Northeast. It is the region's most diversified motorsport publication covering automotive, motorcycle, and veteran's events, and are given out free of charge.

MEMBER SINCE 2004

MY "VETERANS' GARAGE"

1941 WILLYS PICK-UP TRIBUTE GASSER

1933 WILLYS GASSER – "BEYOND NUTS'"

1955 CHEVROLET "210" GASSER

1941 WILLYS COUPE — SBC SUPERCHARGED, 4-SPEED MUNCIE

SHOWS WE HAVE DONE

DISPLAYS WE HAVE BUILT

20. Dropping Meds, Becoming a Runner

FIRST CONTACT WITH VETERANS ADMINISTRATION

Living with PTSD and a wife who was so controlling had a negative effect on my family's well-being. She wouldn't even let my eldest son, Darin, who was her step-son, live with us. Darin ended up living with my mother. Almost every time I would try to have a normal conversation with Margaret, it would escalate into a power struggle. I was always viewed as the lowly bad guy. We had two children together; Marc, a bicentennial baby, born on July 31st, 1976, and Mikael born on August 24th, 1979. Mikael's birthday is also unique. It is exactly 1,900 years to the day that Mount Vesuvius erupted and covered Pompeii, Italy. By 1982 the mental cruelty towards me was getting so bad, I would lose control and start to destroy just about everything in my reach. When I had these temper tantrums, the family would get away as quickly as possible. After a few seconds, I would calm down and wonder what I had just done. It was a release for me and something I just didn't understand. I was threatened by Margaret that she would divorce me if I didn't seek help at the VA. In no uncertain terms would I be away from my boys, so I took her up on it and went to the VA hospital in Newington, Connecticut seeking help. It was the first time I went to the VA since I was discharged from the service in 1967. I explained to a counselor what was happening at home with my out-bursts and how I felt I was being treated. I was diagnosed with a mood disorder and requested that I join a Day-Treatment group for a year. I accepted thinking that if this would save my marriage, I was all for it. While I attended the program, I was able to stay self employed by working weekends and taking care of small repairs after the daily therapy sessions, which ended mid-afternoons. When the year was up, it was suggested that I join a couple's group that would meet once a week for two hours on Tuesday afternoons. I explained the offer to Margaret and she accepted. So for the following year, Margaret and I were part of a round table group of five couples who were also trying to save their relationships. About halfway through the program, one of the counselors took me aside and told me that they were not supposed to recommend divorce as an alternative to helping solve marital problems.

He then told me, "You've got to divorce this woman." I felt that I finally found someone who understood what I was experiencing to make me act the way I was behaving. I knew that in most cases, the custody of the children goes to the mother. I therefore continued to live the way I had been and to tolerate the abuse the best way I knew how. Since I was a work-a-holic, it was a good thing that I was away from home most of the time. I believed I was making the best of it due to the circumstances I was involved with. Margaret and I remained together this way until 1992. She was a celebrity chaser and began seeing a male friend, as she called him, in the southeastern part of the state. They were going together at events to try to meet famous entertainers. She has photos of herself along with the likes of Paul Newman, Geraldo Rivera, Phil Donohue, and Tom Jones, amongst others. It was hard for me to accept what was going on, so I was having repercussions of the past and had to seek out help from the VA hospital again.

MIND ALTERING MEDICATION

I explained to the doctor at the VA what had been going on at home. He suggested and prescribed Prozac would be the drug that I take to help me with my anxiety and mood disorder. I began to take the pills as recommended but immediately found that they weren't for me. It was the first time in my life I ever took anything like this. I woke up on the first morning after taking these and tried to go to work. I was approaching my truck in my driveway, feeling like a zombie. I never felt so held back and being in a stupor such as this. I never took another one of them.

A Fateful Occurrence

That same week that I had the bad experience with the medication, I met a new friend. I explained to her what I was going through and what the meds had done to me.

She quickly responded by saying, "You should try running." I told her I didn't understand. She said it was a great stress reliever and suggested we go out for a run. The next evening, I brought along some sneakers and shorts and ran with her for about a mile and a half. The first time I ran that distance since basic training. I felt a feeling of euphoria, something I hadn't felt before. The run was quite easy for me because I had been running with my twelve-year-old son, Mikael, mornings for the past eight months delivering newspapers on his route. I never realized it, but I was training. Mary, my friend, then suggested that I run in a road-race the following Saturday. It was a low key four-mile foot race held at Manchester Community College. I agreed and showed up, not knowing what I was getting myself into. It was the second week of June,1992, just a few weeks from my forty-eighth birthday.

My First Road Race

I showed up at the college an hour before the race. I changed into the "running" clothes that I brought along with me. I didn't know any better but wearing an old T-shirt, bathing suit, old tennis sneakers, and black socks didn't get it. When it came time to line up, I moved right to the front of the pack. Here I was amongst the top runners of the day. The loud air horn went off, and we were on our way. For the first quarter mile or so, I stayed with the front runners. Then all of a sudden, it was like a ton of bricks had hit me in the chest; I slowed down to a more comfortable pace. My chest hurt for the rest of the race. When I approached the finish line, my name was announced over the speakers that it was my first road race. I got a round of applause that I didn't expect. I then found out that I had taken third place in the forty's division. I won a $15 coupon that was to be exchanged for running gear that was on racks in the gym close by. The singlets and running shorts were at greatly reduced prices and from a popular running store. I picked an ensemble to my liking and was about to leave when I noticed a brand-new pair of Saucony running shoes laying in the grass. I questioned the race promoter who's they were, and he responded that a runner recently purchased them and were not pleased the way they fit. He was selling them for $5. I found that they were my size, so I bought them on the spot. I now had my whole running outfit. I then questioned where you found these races. I was told that they were listed on Fridays in the Hartford Courant sports section.

Before I left, I was approached by a kind young lady who whispered in my ear, "You know, you don't wear black socks with white sneakers." That was the last time I pulled that off! Little did I know that this was to be the beginning of a seventeen-year obsession of competing in long distance road racing.

A RUNNING OBSESSION

I averaged a road race a weekend for the seventeen years I was involved in this sport. I threw in a few cross country and track racing events now and again. I have even run in and completed six marathons, which are just plain brutal. You have to train for at least six months prior, which includes long distance training runs of over fifteen miles. A lot of time is required to be a marathon runner. I am happy to say, by being a competitive runner, it has kept me off of mind-altering medications and helped me ward off the demons associated with having PTSD. After that first road race, I began looking for those weekend races, and there were plenty to be found. Most were 5K (3.1 mile) races, but now and then odd distances were always in the meddle. I was racing every weekend and soon found a couple of runners in my age group that would share the driving duties to and from those races. We also went out during the week days training on the roads or at schools with some of the student athletes. For about a year and a half, if a road race included down-hills, I would suffer greatly. I had the chronic back pain which originated from those jumps out of the Huey helicopters. I ran through the pain, and eventually my back strengthened, so it became more bearable to endure the agony. It always felt good to place first, second, or third in your age bracket in a race, so that is what I would always strive to do. Being at the end of an age division was always tough, so I felt great when I became fifty years of age. In most cases, I was placing in my division in these races. For years I was focused, super healthy, and avoided most PTSD breakdowns. I am so glad I found this alternative treatment to help with my disabilities.

AUTHOR FOUND RUNNING AS THERAPY

AUTHOR SECOND FROM LEFT AT LAKE WINNIPESAUKE 66-MILE RELAY RACE WITH TEAM

AUTHOR ON RIGHT — FOUR GOLD MEDALS AND A BRONZE

At a 5-K road race

AUTHOR WAS A MEMBER OF THE "GRUMPY-BUT FAST-OLD MEN" RELAY TEAM THAT RACED FROM MT. WASHINGTON TO HAMPTON BEACH-200 MILES. WE STILL HOLD THE "OVER 55" RECORD IN UNDER TWELVE HOURS. WE RACED TWO YEARS IN A ROW.

21. Another Divorce, Legal Stealing

Eighteen years I lived with a partner that wasn't on my side. By the end of 1993, we mutually agreed to a divorce. We remained in our home together while the divorce was pending. Our two boys were nearing their graduation from high school. Family Services were holding weekly council meetings with the boys, so they could cope better with our break-up. During this time, I was pressured into losing my temper one day to the point of being completely out of control. Margaret called the police and put all the blame on me. I was ushered to the police station along with my collection of long rifles. A bail was put on my head, and I was immediately locked up. I was given the opportunity to make one phone call. I called my mom and explained the situation I was in. I told her the combination to my safe and pleaded with her to bring the acquired money to the station and bail me out. She did just that. Thank God for moms. I would never, ever want to be locked up ever again. Freedom is such a cherished gift. I never had to go to court or anything. A few days later, I got a call from the police department requesting that I pick up my personal property, my rifles. It must have been quite a sight to see, me walking down the street with the six rifles I had clutched in my arms. I don't think that would be allowed today.

LIVING UP TO A REPUTATION

About a year prior to the divorce, I was driving my car late in the afternoon on Main Street, Middletown to meet a client of mine to present him with an estimate for new replacement windows for his rental property. I was stopped

at a traffic light and noticed a young lady across the street walking in the opposite direction. She happened to be wearing shorts and was the harbinger of
spring. The driver behind me, in a huge soft-drink beverage truck, noticed
her, too. As I pulled away from the light, when it turned green, a lady offered
me her parking spot, which was to the immediate right-front of me. I stopped
abruptly to let her back out, and before I could blink, the beverage truck
climbed right over the trunk of my car. When the twenty-eight-year-old driver
of the truck was questioned, he responded by saying that he had his eyes on
the spring chicken. An ambulance was called, and I was taken to the local hospital for observation. The insurance companies monitored the case, and I was
appointed an attorney from Hartford, Connecticut. I spoke to him once about
the facts of the accident, and he put my file in his cabinet at his office. A few
months went by when I unexpectedly received a call from Leo, my attorney
for the accident case. He informed me that he received a call from the beverage
company and they offered to settle with me for the sum of $100,000. They
did not want to go through litigations. Leo recommended that I take the offer
considering the history of my past. I agreed to go ahead with the offer. Three
days later, Leo called again stating that he received the check and he would
take out his one third fee and bring me a check for the remainder. I argued a
little with him saying that he only filed my case away in his office. It was a no-
win situation. He rounded off the payment, including the documentation or
paperwork fees, and within an hour of the phone call, brought me a check for
the sum of $66,000. I signed all the papers releasing the beverage company
from any further claims. I never heard from or saw Leo ever again. Margaret
and her attorney heard of the settlement payment that I had received. Within
a couple days, I received notice of a deposition for our divorce that I would
have to attend at her attorney's office located just off Main Street in Hartford,
Connecticut. Her attorney was a twenty-eight-year-old female recently graduated from law school. From what I noticed, she was trying to impress her two
uncles who owned the law firm. The day I attended the deposition, it was requested that I bring along the settlement check from my accident with the
beverage company. I was a little taken aback when I entered the conference
room at the firm's office. My attorney was seated at the right end of a ten-foot-
long table. My wife was at the opposite end. I seated myself down in the center
facing my wife's attorney on the left and her two uncles who were seated just
to the right of her. I felt that I was about to be raked over the coals. One of

the uncles asked if I brought the settlement check along with me. I said yes as I laid it on the table in front of me. I don't remember too much about the deposition, except when my attorney questioned Carrie, my wife's attorney, what she was charging Mrs. Augustine for the divorce.

She was squinting as she looked at the check and slowly responded, "$33,000."

Without a beat, my attorney, Lloyd, responded with, "That is my fee." The check was quickly removed from the table. And this is legal, my friend. A month later, I attended my divorce hearing. I was promptly made out to be the bad guy. By the laws of the state of Connecticut, our marital possessions were split fifty-fifty. I felt like I had been totally defeated. All the mental cruelty I lived with the past eighteen years and all the effort I put into to get ahead in life, being a work-a-holic was all for naught I thought. I moved on, continually working, racing, and training daily, which helped to keep my PTSD at a somewhat comfortable level. I soon met a wonderful young lady who was an avid tennis player. She worked in human resources at a large industrial firm in Hartford. She became my significant other, moved in with me, and eventually we became engaged. We enjoyed traveling and going to the road races together. She would even compete now and then when she was up for it. Six years into our relationship, my mother passed on. While I was attending probate court for my mom's estate, I found out that my sister hired two attorneys to help her contest the will. It soon became a fiasco. My mother had left everything she owned to my eldest son. My mother's will was rock solid. The probate hearings took all of fourteen months because of the lame requests by my sister's attorneys. They knew all the dirty tricks to prolong the case. A prominent Connecticut state senator who was also an attorney, was appointed to manage, watch-over, calculate, and submit monthly financial reports of my mother's estate to the I.R.S. Since my son had been my life-long dependent, I was given the task to collect all the monthly financial dealings of my mother's estate and present them to the senator, so he could arrange them in an appropriate form to be submitted. Well, since my fiancé worked at human resources, this type of work just happened to be what she was accustomed to. So for the fourteen months while the probate hearings were going on, Terri, my fiancé, graciously performed the work that was supposed to be done by the senator/attorney. Each month we dropped off the completed financial statements and forms at his house in Wethersfield, Connecticut. He didn't have to do a thing. I have to mention two other things about this senator/attorney that I am not happy with. He shirked his duty during the whole course of the probate hearings. While overlooking the case, the estate taxes were to be paid within nine months of my mother's death. I mentioned this at one of the early hearings. He responded with a statement saying that the taxes would be paid at the conclusion of the hearings. Well, his responsibilities just weren't taken care of. Nine months into the hearings, I received a penalty bill from the I.R.S. for $19,600 for not paying the estate taxes on time. And that fee was in addition to the taxes that were later paid. There was also an included statement that warned me if the taxes were not paid within a few days, a horrendous interest would be tacked on. I abruptly sent in the check for the full amount. Thank you, senator. During one of the hearings, my ex-wife Margaret showed up to plead her case. When put on the stand, she immediately began to chastise my character. She also falsely stated that my mother promised to leave her sons a substantial inheritance. She was suddenly ushered out of the hearing. Fourteen months went by, and we were attending the final hearing. My sister was there with her two attorneys. A new judge from New Haven was appointed to the case. I was getting frustrated and was thinking that this case could go on forever. I made an offer of $65,000 to be paid to my sister, who reluctantly accepted as a result of the prodding by her attorneys. It was quite a while before I saw a similar smile that was on the face of my sister's attorneys. My sister was soon committed to a convalescent home as a ward of the state by her attorneys. Her attorneys walked away with their $65,000 fee. And it was legal?

Icing on the Cake

A couple of weeks after the final hearing of my mom's probate, I received the financial report and the conclusive findings. There in the paperwork was a receipt that showed that Paul, the senator/attorney, had been paid his fee of $10,000. And it was legal? I happened to be running in a road race the following spring and noticed another runner that looked familiar. It was Paul, the senator/attorney. He spotted me and turned red in the face. I was in line about to obtain my post-race snacks when I was trying to get his attention. He disappeared, and I was unable to find him for the rest of the event. His responsibilities of his duty to serve honorably during my mother's probate was so corrupt, it bothered me for quite some time. I eventually submitted a complaint with the state attorney's office, grievance committee. My complaint was accepted and a hearing was scheduled. Well, wouldn't you know it, he brought along another attorney to the hearing, and between them they manipulated the facts to a degree that my complaint was dropped. I recently read an article in the newspaper praising the senator to the point that he is receiving a humanitarian award. When I read that, it really got my goat. How can he sleep nights?

22. 1,576 Steps – Another Eight-Year Quest

In the summer of 1995, my running friend and competitor, Dave Jacobs, suggested that I enter the Empire State Building Run-Up. I had been competing in road racing along with Dave for three years and trusted him. I took him up on his offer and questioned him as to what was involved. He explained to me that I would have to send in an interesting resume of my running history and health to the New York Road Runners Club no sooner than Thanksgiving Day for the following February competition. Dave had competed in the race for eleven years, so he was quite knowledgeable on the subject. He then informed me that hundreds apply, and I would be lucky if I was chosen to be one of the approximately 150 that were allowed to compete. I was also informed that once you are chosen, you would be allowed to compete annually if you so choose. The following is a manuscript I wrote and submitted in an annual writing contest at our local library. The subject was to be about an "adventure." I was awarded a second place.

"I've made the trip eight times on the Metro in New Haven during February from 1996 through 2002 and again in 2007. The train took me to Grand Central Station where I disembarked with my little gym bag and walked twenty-one blocks to 34th Street and Fifth Avenue where the Empire State Building stands. I was committed to run (ESBRU), or the Empire State Building Run-Up, and win my division. ESBRU is a world-wide invitational race put on annually by the New York Road Runners Club. Over 2,000 athletes enter annually submitting a resume of their athletic and running history. Approximately 150 competitors are chosen out of the entrance submissions on the basis of their backgrounds. I submitted my resume during Thanksgiving week prior to the February 1996 competition. It was the first time I entered. I was fortunate to be chosen to compete. The race would consist of running 1,576 stairs, or eighty-six floors of the world-famous building. I became a competitive runner just three and a half years prior at the age of forty-seven, when giving up medications and finding an alternate method to relieve stress. I had been running in road races weekly, so was in prime shape to enter the competition, or so I thought. February 22nd, 1996 came too soon. I boarded the 7 A.M. Metro Line in New haven like a child on his first day of school. As I was riding to Grand Central, my mind was in a state of wonderment, filled with questions, such as, *What did I get myself into, did I train enough? Am I up to competing with these world-class athletes?* When I arrived in the lobby of the Empire State Building, I was abruptly guided to the basement where I was greeted by a tall fellow in a George Washington costume. It was Washington's birthday. A King Kong likeness was also mingling in the crowd of competitors. Before we knew it, we were ushered to the starting line on the first floor. I was amazed by the media positioned nearby. Cameras, bright lights, and reporters were there to capture the event. I found myself in the middle of the pack as the younger runners were fighting for position to be closer to the starting line. When the air-horn went off, it was mass hysteria. Through the flashing lights and roar of the crowd, I literally was carried the thirty feet down the hall to the doorway of the stairwell. As we tried to funnel through the doorway, I could hear screams of pain from runners who were bruised and elbowed. When I started to ascend the first staircase, I quickly learned that one step at a time would burn me out. With leaps and bounds, two steps at a time was the way to go. I also discovered that pulling myself up by the railings enhanced my performance. Besides the approximate 172 landings, there were three hallways to run down, accessing new staircases. Water stations were located in these hallways. Runners had to be careful not to slip and fall or run into custodians who were mopping up all the spilled water. Paper cups were strewn everywhere. Each floor that we came upon had a stenciled number on its entrance door. The rules specified that we could exit the race at any time if we felt ill or were unable to make it to the finish. As I made my way up the stairs, concentrating on my form and speed, running full boar, I happened to glance at an entrance door. It read Number 37. I was spent, totally exhausted, and hurting. I didn't want to think that there were fifty more floors to climb. *Is this where the second wind is supposed to kick in?* I thought. From here-on, it became mind-over-matter. My throat was raw due to the breathing in of the dust being kicked up, plus the higher we ascended, the hotter it became. Heat rises. Another thing I'll never forget was when an exit door opened abruptly on one of the upper floors. Two custodians were there, leaning on their brooms, looking curiously into the stairwell at the commotion. As I was going by, our eyes met, and their expressions changed from curiosity to a look of horror. It was if they had just met the craziest person on earth running up the stairs. I don't think they were aware that there was a race going on. When I did make it through the finish line and collapsed against a wall, after a few minutes of gasping for air and recuperating, I began to search for the results print-out. I finished the race in fourteen minutes and fifty-eight seconds, second place in the fifty-year-old division, twenty-ninth overall out of the 150-plus runners. That experience sparked a desire to continue to compete annually in the ESBRU. In 2001, my sixth year of competing, I traveled to Las Vegas to train in a tall building, something I never had done. It was a week before ESBRU. I stayed at the Hilton Hotel. Each morning for a week, I woke up at 6:30 A.M. and ran three heats of the thirty-eight floors as fast as I was able. My hard work paid off. Each day my elapsed times improved. My sixth attempt at ESBRU had finally arrived. It was the year that the most competitors in my division would compete, eighteen. When I warmed up on the long staircase from the basement to the first floor, I immediately knew that I would have not only a good race but a great one. I was in terrific condition. Low and behold, this was my day. I finally won the fifty-year-old division at fifty-five-years-old. I was truly elated to win a world-class competition. Over the eight years that I competed in ESBRU, I was able to place second four times, third three times, and winning the division once. This certainly has been quite an adventure."

I had been told by fellow competitors that if you can run to the top of this building in under fifteen minutes, you are of Olympic caliber. I am proud to say I've done it four times in my fifties.

On February 19th, 1998, my third attempt at ESBRU, I ran my quickest time, 14:28. I was able to defeat the following: 1st place runner from the NY Fire Dept. age 32, 14:39; 1st place runner from Mexico, age 27, 14:45; 1st place runner from Canada, age 26, 15:02; 1st NY Police Dept. age 40, 15:17.

I must admit, the success I have had in the ESBRU competitions was due to thirty years of being a roofer. I constantly carried eighty to one-hundred-pound materials up ladders throughout my career. The labor made my legs super-strong. The physical work also kept me in tip-top shape.

Race Name, Date	Finisher Name	Gender/ Age	City, State	Team	Distance (miles)	Gun Time	Net Time	Pace/ Mile	Overall Place	Gender Place	Age Place
Empire State Building Run-Up February 6, 2007	Augustine, Jerry	M61	Middletown, CT		.2		16:57		105	88	3
Empire State Building Run-up February 5, 2002	Augustine, Jerry	M56	Middletown, CT	HTC	.2	15:35			52	48	3
Empire State Building Run-up February 7, 2001	Augustine, Jerry	M55	Middletown, CT		.2	15:18			47	41	1
Empire State Building Run-up February 23, 2000	Augustine, Jerry	M54	Middletown, CT	HTC	.2	14:53			41	37	2
Empire State Building Run-Up February 25, 1999	Augustine, Jerry	M53		HTC	.0	15:19			53	48	3
Empire State Building Run-Up February 19, 1998	Augustine, Jerry	M52		HTC	.2	14:28			31	29	2
Empire State Building Run-Up February 20, 1997	Augustine, Jerry	M51		MOHE	.2	14:50			38	35	2
Empire State Building Run-Up February 22, 1996	Augustine, Jerry	M50		MOHE	.2	14:58			36	29	2

ARCHIVES OF NEW YORK ROAD RUNNERS CLUB

AUTHOR AT EMPIRE STATE BUILDING RUN-UP WITH WINNERS' MEDAL

AUTHOR IN LOBBY JUST PRIOR TO ESBRU 2007

AUTHOR WITH "KING KONG" AND DAVE JACOBS
FIRST YEAR RUNNING ESBRU

EMPIRE STATE BUILDING RUN-UP: Jerry Augustine, 55, of Middletown was the top finisher in the 50-59 age group in this year's run up the stairs of the Empire State building in New York City.

Augustine completed the race from the first floor to the observation deck (86 floors and 1,576 steps) in 15:18. He was 39th overall of the 116 male finishers. Nearly 200 participated.

Augustine is a memebr of the Middletown YMCA and the Hartford Track Club.

FEB 24 2001

LOCAL PAPER ARTICLE

AUTHOR WITH RUNNING FRIEND AND ESBRU COMPETITOR

23. Summer Biathlon

I had been well into competing in long distance road racing every weekend in the mid 1990's. I was reading the Hartford Courant newspaper one morning when something caught my eye. There was a small add for a competition, which was to be held at an Army national guard post just outside of Providence, Rhode Island. The event was called Summer Biathlon. It was sponsored by Marlin Fire Arms, who supplied the five-shot, bolt action, biathlon rifles. The sport was formed so the winter biathlon competitors would have a way to train and compete in the spring, summer, and fall months. The Winter Biathlon rules stated that the entrant carry their rifle slung over their shoulder while they skied to the shooting range. In Summer Biathlon, the entrant ran the course and would slow down to a walk to retrieve his rifle at a rack and walk to the range to fire his shots. In most cases, the event was comprised of running one mile, stopping to shoot five shots in the prone position, returning the rifle to the rack, running another mile and shooting five shots off-hand (standing), and then running the final mile to the finish line. I was pretty much intrigued as to what I read, so I got into my car at around 5 A.M. the following Sunday morning and headed out for the eighty-five miles to a new adventure in my fifty-year-old body. I arrived at the East Greenwich, Rhode Island post with a general idea of knowing what I was getting myself into. First of all, all those that were to compete had to attend a safety class to earn a Summer Biathlon registration card. I was amongst the thirty-five who were there to learn the basic rules, and more importantly, how to handle a weapon safely. Some were repeat attendees. The running course and shooting range were confined right on the post. The cross-country trail that we ran on was well-packed dirt without a hill in it. The targets consisted of black, metal round discs, the size of soft-balls that would flip over, turning white, if they were hit. They were placed twenty-five meters from the shooter. During idle chat, it was mentioned that the overall winner from the previous year was a twenty-eight-year-old Rhode Island State Trooper. He showed up about twenty minutes before the start. I had a great advantage in this type of competition. I was so used to running in races, so this was right up my alley. The only thing I had to be careful with this time was the shooting aspect. For every miss of the target, fifteen seconds was added to your overall time. When you approached the firing line, you were still breathing pretty heavily from running the mile all out. You had to be careful and make sure to pull the trigger when your siting fell on the target. It is difficult to say the least. I happened to hit all my targets, ten out of ten, and I ran damn well. I won the whole event outright. The trooper missed a couple targets and was proclaimed second place winner. It was close. This experience sparked another desire to compete in more of these exciting competitions. I joined the Summer Biathlon association and was on my way to compete in as many of these races that I could fit into my running schedule. I told my good friend, Mike Chowaniec, about this new adventure that I was now involved in, and he just so happened to own an Anschutz biathlon rifle, the premier rifle of this sport. Mike graciously lent me his rifle for the duration of all my competitions. Another Summer Biathlon event came up at a Shooting Sport Camp at Marlborough, Massachusetts. I not only won my age group, but I won the race overall. That was truly a cross-country course to run on. There were streams, rocks, hills and narrow trails to run; it was quite difficult. The more I competed in the Summer Biathlons, the more competitive I became. I traveled to Cherry Hill, New Jersey, central Pennsylvania, Mount Holyoke and Westover Airforce Base, Massachusetts, A New Ipswich, New Hampshire shooting-sport camp, Rhode Island, Wallingford, Connecticut, and many other places that could handle an event such as this. My girlfriend Terri accompanied me to the race at Cherry Hill, New Jersey. I talked her into competing by saying it would be more fun to join in than to just sit around for a few hours as a spectator. Little did we know that it was a five-mile race inclusive of three shooting stops. I didn't hear the end of it on the long drive home late that afternoon. We were spent. The distances and rules varied at all the races. Sometimes you had to run a penalty lap at a predetermined distance for every target miss. At some races, you didn't have to place your rifle back in the rack after shooting. In most cases, the penalties were time added on to your total. The highlight of my Summer Biathlon career came when I traveled to Lake Placid, New York along with my teenaged son, Mikael, to compete in the Summer Biathlon Festival. We competed on the same course as the 1980 Winter Olympics. It was a two-day event where we slept and ate at the Mt. Hoevenberg Olympic Sports Complex. We even got to take a ride in the 55 M.P.H. bobsled and got to visit the Lake Placid Winter Olympic Museum where the U.S. team defeated the Russians in the 1980 Winter Olympics. We got to wear a competitors I.D. and lanyard around our necks, which got us into every attraction for the whole weekend. I have many fond memories of this sport. I am so glad I was a part of it.

AUTHOR AT SUMMER BIATHLON COMPETITION

AUTHOR IN COMPETITION FIRING ANSCHUTZ RIFLE

AUTHOR AT BIATHLON RANGE

AUTHOR AT WESTOVER AIRBASE SUMMER BIATHLON WITH GIRLFRIEND

SONS, MIKAEL AND MARC FIRING PRONE

MIKAEL AND MARC ON THE STARTING LINE

AUTHOR WITH SONS AT SUMMER BIATHLON, WALLINGFORD, CT

24. 2010 Joining Veterans' Groups

In 2010 I was thinking back to my past and what I had accomplished in life and what was in store for me in the future. I built my new hobby garage, Veteran's Garage, in 2006 and retired from being self-employed in 2007. I was still using running and athletics as therapy to treat my PTSD symptoms. I joined the Greater Middletown Military Museum as a lifetime member. I knew that Middletown was a city with a wealth of historical element and information. I had the desire to be a part of it. I was already a charter member of the Middlesex County Historical Society Car Show committee. I had been volunteering for over thirty years to help make our annual antique car and truck show a success. Joining the committee of the museum brought me in contact with many local veterans that were members of the many veterans' organizations in my community. I joined our local Veterans of the Vietnam War; The American Legion, post 75, Catholic War Veterans, post 1166, VFW, (Veterans of Foreign Wars), post 1840, which recently became united with post 583, and the DAV (Disabled American Veterans), chapter #7. Being a member of these organizations automatically allowed you to attend the monthly meetings of the Counsel of Veterans, which is a unique organization in our city that oversees the operations of the local veterans organizations. The Counsel of Veterans also manages our annual Memorial Day parade and the events that take place during Veterans Day week. During the past ten years, I became more and more involved with these veterans groups. I have held numerous positions and am presently Chaplain of all of them, except the Counsel of Veterans, of which I am assistant Chaplain. Some of my duties include reading the prayers at veterans' wakes and interments. I read the opening and closing prayers at the veterans meetings. I also read the invocations and benedictions at the Memorial Day and Veterans Day ceremonies at the Connecticut State Veterans Cemetery, which is located in our city. I am presently the commander of DAV chapter #7 where I open and close the meeting and follow "Robert's Rules of Order," which governs the method of managing the meeting. I am very honored to be associated with these veterans groups and will remain to be of help as long as I am able. I recently became a member of B.P.O.E. Elks' #771 of Middletown, Connecticut and am honored to belong to this well-respected fellowship.

VETERANS HELPING VETERANS

In 2010 it was suggested to me to visit the Hartford, Connecticut Vet Center where I could meet up with fellow veterans to discuss their experiences that are similar to mine. It is a federally funded institution but not associated with the VA hospital. It has been ranked third in the country for service to our veterans. I went there and joined one of the eighteen round table discussion groups that meet once a week for one and a half hours. Many veterans who have been traumatized during their "tour of duty," whether it be by combat or by other means, have been helped through the many programs at the center. Combat veterans who have been emotionally inflicted have been helped immensely there and returned to a more meaningful degree of a normal lifestyle. Some of the issues that are covered there are as follows: Educational, financial, legal, medical, psychological, social, and vocational. It has been a great resource for me and for other veterans to find comradeship with others who have experienced the same form of military service in their life.

An interesting coincidence was discovered during one of the roundtable discussions. Forty-five years prior when Nancy Sinatra visited our newly finished Tay Ninh base camp, I just so happened to take a picture of her performance. In the photo was the back of the head of James Natale, who also served with the 196th, and is a member of our round table. We had a good laugh.

I still converse with them on a daily basis. The companionship we have mustered will, no doubt be a part of us for the rest of our lives.

**GREATER MIDDLETOWN MILITARY MUSEUM
BUILDING COMMITTEE**

MAYOR DANIEL T. DREW

COMMITTEE CHAIRMAN: COUNCILMAN ROBERT S. BLANCHARD

KENNETH A. MCCLELLAN (US ARMY, RET.)
RON ORGANEK (US ARMY, RET.)
JERRY AUGUSTINE (US ARMY)
MICHAEL ROGALSKY (US ARMY)

PHILIP CACCIOLA (US ARMY, RET.)
LAWRENCE RILEY (US AIR FORCE)
EDWARD MONARCA (US ARMY, N.G)
ARTHUR MEYERS (US ARMY)

STAFF TO THE COMMITTEE
CHRISTOPHER M. HOLDEN, P.E, MIDDLETOWN DPW

ARCHITECT
STEVEN NELSON, MPN ARCHITECTS

GENERAL CONTRACTOR
J A ROSA CONSTRUCTION LLC

APRIL 13, 2019

AUTHOR ON BUILDING COMMITTEE, GMMM

AWARDED PLAQUE

PAST COMMANDER OF VVW

AUTHOR AT DEDICATION WITH LOCAL SCOUTS

PATCHES ON AUTHOR'S DAV JACKET

AUTHOR CMDR. CHPT. 7 2020-2021

HARTFORD VET CENTER, ROCKY HILL, CT

MY ORIGINAL WEEKLY MORNING GROUP

VETERANS GARAGE PICNIC

AUTHOR WITH HIS CO. CMDR. AT REUNION 2005

Cassandra Day / Hearst Connectic

Chaplain and Vietnam veteran Jerry Augustine, a member of the American Legion Post 75 and Veterans of Vietam Wars in Middletown, gives the invocation during the groundbreaking ceremony for the State Veterans Cemetery expansion and improvements projects.

INVOCATION - AUTHOR AT CT STATE VETERANS CEMETERY

At CSVC.

Laying of Wreath on Memorial Day

MURAL WALL DEDICATION AT CITY HALL

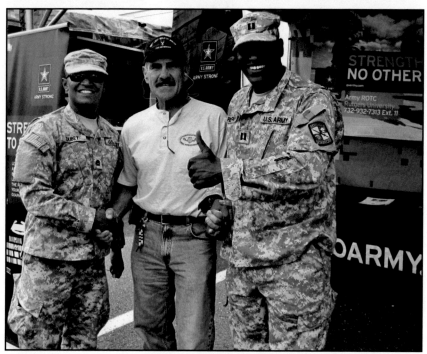

HONORED BY "ARMY-OF-ONE" IN 2010
WON ALL DAY PUSH-UP CONTEST ELIZABETHTOWN, NJ

25. Agent Orange Will Never Go Away

"One of the terrible legacies of the Vietnam war is what many veterans believe to be their contamination with Agent Orange. Used as an herbicide and sprayed by the U. S, Air Force from C-123 aircraft in a defoliation operation called Ranch Hand from 1962-1970. This chemical contained minute amounts (approximately 2.0 parts per million) of a poisonous substance called 2,3,7,8-tetrachloridibenzo-para-dioxin, (TCDD), a type of dioxin, which has been claimed to result in various health problems." Some of the most heavily sprayed were inland forests of the junction of the borders of Cambodia, Laos, and South Vietnam, and the inland forests north and northwest of Saigon, exactly where my tour of duty took place. The last spraying of the herbicides by airplanes were carried out in January of 1971. The last by helicopter or on the ground were terminated by the end of 1971. All total 18.85 million gallons of the herbicides were sprayed in areas that were potentially occupied by our ground troops. The primary use of the dioxin was to kill vegetation and thereby deny cover to enemy forces. Soldiers came in contact with the defoliant as they moved through jungle areas and also from drinking the water from streams and brooks that had been contaminated. Beginning in the late 1970's, Vietnam veterans began to cite Dioxin as the cause of health problems ranging from skin rashes to cancer to birth defects in their children. What I had mentioned previously were the symptoms I had developed due to my contact with AO while serving in combat. Besides the rash, or jungle rot as we called it, I developed recurring boils and skin lesions soon after I returned home. A few years ago, I was diagnosed as having Malignant Melanoma and subsequently had my twenty-eight lymphnodes removed from my right axilla. I am periodically monitored by the dermatology clinic at the VA hospital. Hopefully my cancer remains in remission. I am presently taking seven medications to treat my other ailments, high blood pressure, high cholesterol, bladder, and prostate problems.

Dioxin Effects on my Offspring

Not only that I had been affected by these criminal acts, as they are now known to be, they have also affected the lives of my children. Not one of my three sons have ever worked at a meaningful job. My eldest son, Darin, who is 100 percent disabled, is constantly being monitored and treated at hospitals throughout the northeast. There isn't a day that goes by that he is not suffering from his disabilities related to AO. He also has Asperger's Syndrome.

His latest test result that was administered by the Genome Medical Clinic the first week of March 2021 reads as follows, "You were found to have one likely disease-causing variant that indicates you are a carrier of a recessive condition. You are a carrier of autosomal recessive infantile liver failure and autosomal recessive SOPH Syndrome. Carriers are not expected to have symptoms but can be at an increased risk to have an affected child. No disease-causing, (pathogenic), variants identified. Your recurrent fevers of unclear origin and recurrent pericarditis may represent a diagnosis caused by a gene not included in the panel completed, or may not yet have an associated genetic cause." The tests that were ordered and administered were as follows: Autoinflammatory, syndromes panel with add-on autoimmunity genes, primary immunodeficiency, and panel, nephrolithiasis panel.

My middle son, Marc, committed suicide in 2014 at the age of thirty-eight. He was a brilliant scholar and college graduate who also was affected with skin disorders and mental health issues. He was diagnosed with having P.T.S.D. He had to be treated with "heavy" medications.

My youngest son, Mikael, also a college graduate, suffers from Schizophrenia and refuses to leave the house. He lives with my ex-wife, Margaret, and has periodically been hospitalized due to his suicidal tendencies.

I am sure my son's health issues were caused by AO through me. The most devastating effect that the spraying of AO has on me is that my desire to be a grand-parent will remain to be unfulfilled. Not one of my sons ever had the desire to become a parent. I will never be allowed to share any future successes of my children or grandchildren.

I am honored to have been chosen, as the chaplain who has read the invocation and benediction at the ceremony of the installation of the Agent Orange Monument that was held at the junction of rt.6 and rt. 316 in Andover, Connecticut on June 11th, 2021.

My son, Marc's headstone

26. Best Conditioned Chaplain in the VFW

In 2017 I got a call from Kari Williams, an editorial associate of VFW Magazine. Someone had contacted her and suggested that I would be a good candidate for the monthly article, "Vets in Focus * Inspiring Profiles of Extraordinary Veterans." She graciously requested an interview of my military history that would be edited and published in an upcoming issue of the magazine. It was an honor to be recognized and chosen to be part of this fine military publication, so I happily agreed. The following article was published in the January 2018 issue.

The Best-Conditioned Chaplain in the VFW

A Vietnam vet turned to bodybuilding and running to placate the 'wicked' effects of PTSD. He's since earned titles in both sports.

BY KARI WILLIAMS

andbags and a bamboo stick. That's how Vietnam veteran Jerry Augustine stayed in shape overseas. And it helped lead him to a bodybuilding journey that culminated with the honors of Mr. New England and Mr. Northeast America in 1975.

Augustine served in Vietnam from Aug. 4, 1966 to Aug. 4, 1967. He initially was with the 3rd Bn., 21st Inf., 196th Light Inf. Bde., and was transferred to the 2nd Bn., 12th Inf., 4th Inf. Div., after seven months. A friend from the Army suggested that Augustine try bodybuilding because he "had good potential."

"I just loved the competition," Augustine said, "and when I came out of Vietnam, I just had these goals that I had to do. I had to be the best at something. I think it was because we didn't get the recognition when we came home from Vietnam."

Augustine, who served as a combat infantryman, said he was "really wired up" after returning stateside. He worked at his father's roofing company and lifted weights in the evening.

He competed professionally for eight years, ending his bodybuilding career with the victories as Mr. New England and Mr. Northeast America. His focus then shifted to the family roofing business, which he bought from his father. In 1981, Augustine was diagnosed with a mood disorder and underwent "day treatment" for two years at the Newington (Conn.) VA Hospital.

"PTSD had a real wicked effect on me," said Augustine, who has been married and divorced three times. "It wasn't good [for] my family life, and I became like a walking time bomb almost."

VFW member Jerry Augustine uses running as a way to combat symptoms of PTSD. He began competing in the Empire State Building Run-Up in 1996, winning first place in the 50-59-year-old division in 2001.

During his first week in Vietnam, while on ambush patrol, he fell into a backyard well.

Another time, Augustine was nearly hit by a rifle-propelled grenade that hit a tree and bounced on his boot.

"That should've killed me right on the spot," Augustine said.

His unit also was at the Battle of Dau Tang while attached to the 1st Infantry Division. One of Augustine's jobs was to put fallen soldiers in body bags.

"[The] night that we did that, we had to go into the jungle where the battle was, we had to stay in their positions ...

[There was] blood all over the ground, trees were all just chopped up, everything chopped up and then the smell of death," Augustine said.

Doctors, according to Augustine, prescribed him Prozac in 1992, which made him "so lethargic" he could not work.

"A friend who was from a family that competed in running in road races suggested that I try running to relieve stress," Augustine said. "I immediately ran that evening, something I had never done except basic training, and I felt a relief."

Every weekend for 17 years, beginning in 1992, Augustine competed in a race, ranging from 5Ks to marathons.

"When I got into running, it seemed like every road race, I had to do the best I could," Augustine said.

Then in 1996, at 50 years old, he entered the Empire State Building Run-Up — a race up 86 flights of stairs in the 1,250-foot-tall building. Augustine earned second place with a time of 14:58.

He competed in the run-up regularly, consistently placing second or third and keeping his times between 14:28 and 15:03. In 2001, he won the 50-59 age division with a time of 15:18, competing against 18 others in the division. Augustine spent time training in Las Vegas at the Hilton Hotel, running its 38 flights of stairs in preparation for the first-place victory.

He competed again in 2002, placing third in his division, and in 2007, he secured third place in the 60s division.

Augustine's athletic accomplishments also earned him a place in the Middletown (Conn.) Sports Hall of Fame.

He currently is a chaplain for five organizations, including VFW Post 1840 in Middletown, Conn., and the American Legion.

EMAIL *kwilliams@vfw.org*

VFW member Jerry Augustine once held the bodybuilding competition titles of Mr. New England and Mr. Northeast America. After returning from Vietnam, Augustine began an eight-year bodybuilding career that ended with those victories in 1975. He began competitive running in 1992 and earned titles in that sport, too.

AUTHOR WITH SONS ACCEPTING "HALL OF FAME AWARD.

27. A New Found Passion

In the early fall of 2017, I was approached by Tom Goglia, my friend and fellow member of the DAV Chapter #7. He asked me if I would be interested in competing in a kayak race on the Connecticut River. It was to be a benefit event to help veterans. I told him that I had never been in a kayak, but if they needed more participants, I would be happy to help. The six-mile race took place at the Rocky Hill, Connecticut boat launch landing, also home of the oldest, "still operating," ferry in the nation. When I showed up at the race, I explained that I was new at this, so I was partnered up with an experienced competitor and would race in a double kayak. Not only did we win the "doubles division," we took second overall in the whole race. The competitor that I am, this sparked another desire to continue to partake in this sport. Through the winter months, I trained on "Concept-2" indoor rowing machines, along with disabled veterans who were treating their ills with physical therapy. I also volunteered as a driver to pick up the group of participants at their homes and return them when the sessions were over. I enjoyed the exercising so much on the rowing machines that I purchased my own. I found the movements encountered to be a total body workout. By the spring of 2018, I was competing in indoor rowing competitions and was handily winning my age group division.

WORLD BRONZE MEDAL

In February of 2019, I traveled to the University of Boston to compete in the World Indoor Rowing Championships. I was a little disappointed when I arrived for the competition. Here I was, a seventy-three-year-old, and the eldest division available that I would compete in was the fifty-year-old and older. Meters were attached to the rowing machines that let you know what position you were in as you rowed. When there were two minutes left to row during my event, I noticed I was in fifth place. It was deeply etched in my mind that I wasn't going home without a medal. I let it all hang out and finished earning a bronze medal placing third in the over fifty division. The winner was fifty-four, and the second-place finisher had just turned fifty a couple weeks before. I was elated that all the training that I had done paid off.

AMERICAN AND WORLD RECORD

July 20th, 2019, nine days before my seventy-fourth birthday. I find myself on a Concept-2 rowing machine establishing a new over seventy-year-old, American and World Record time, rowing 6,000 meters. It felt as though I was competing in my younger days.

CO-FOUNDING VETERANS' KAYAKING PROGRAM

In 2020, along with my friend and fellow veteran, Morty Pear, and with the sponsorship of B.P.O.E. Elk's #771 of Middletown, Connecticut, I co-founded the Elk's Veterans' Kayaking Program, which is dedicated to providing a better life-style for disabled veterans and their families. The program runs from May until October on lake-front property that is donated by Sam Babcock, a Vietnam veteran, and is totally free and run by volunteers.

FORCED MARCH FOR SUICIDE PREVENTION

In 2020, for the second time in two years, I joined the 40th Marine Detachment to hike fourteen miles in honor of my son Marc, who I lost to suicide in 2014. At 5:30 A.M., we began our 22K forced march from the Elk's Pavilion in South Glastonbury, Connecticut. The hike is a benefit for the prevention of an average of the twenty-two suicides daily that takes place among our veterans. It is sponsored by Monaco Ford of Glastonbury, Connecticut. The American Legion of Glastonbury was gracious enough to provide breakfast at 8:30 A.M.

during a break. All safety measures were in place during this time of the pandemic. The six-hour trek on the very hilly course is not an easy one. The classic rock music and the camaraderie of the veterans marching, truly helps to get you to the finish. I am proud to say I was the eldest of the finishers at seventy-five. I am also proud to say my friend, Betty Pear, age sixty-seven, finished alongside me.

AUTHOR AT 22K MARCH FOR SUICIDE PREVENTION

ELK'S VETERANS' KAYAKING PROGRAM

AUTHOR- FIRST TIME IN KAYAK -WINS DOUBLES RACE

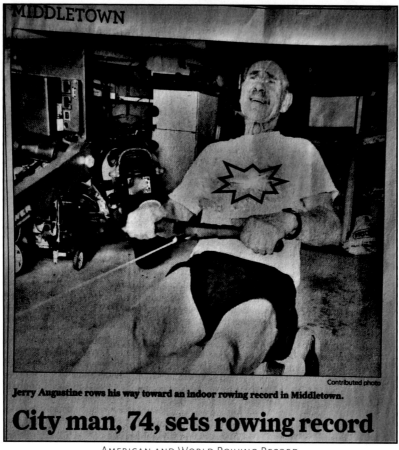

MIDDLETOWN

Contributed photo

Jerry Augustine rows his way toward an indoor rowing record in Middletown.

City man, 74, sets rowing record

AMERICAN AND WORLD ROWING RECORD

AUTHOR AT WORLD INDOOR ROWING CHAMPIONSHIP-BOSTON

AUTHOR RECEIVES BRONZE MEDAL AT WORLD CHAMPIONSHIPS

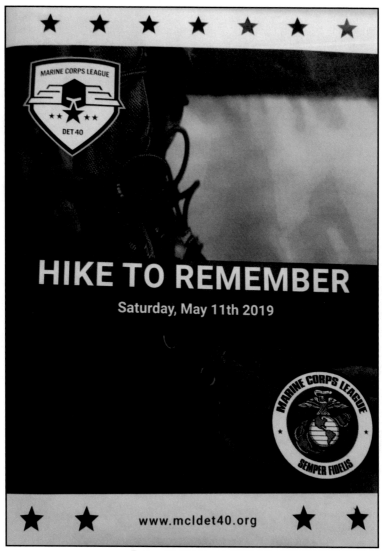

For suicide prevention

22K HIKE (14 MILES)

THE HILLS WERE TOUGH

TOWN SUPPORT

AMERICAN & WORLD ROWING RECORD

28. Veteran of the Year Award

In 2020 I was honored in my county as being the veteran of the year.

Middlesex COUNTY Chamber of COMMERCE

William J. Pomfret Veteran Community Service Award

The William J. Pomfret Veteran Community Service Award is presented annually to a Veteran of the United States Armed Forces, in recognition of his or her distinguished service to the citizens of Connecticut, and selfless commitment to public service.

The 2020 Recipient is Gerald E. "Jerry" Augustine of Middletown.

Jerry Augustine is a native of Middletown, CT. He graduated from Woodrow Wilson High School in 1963, and went on to study at Central Connecticut State University and the University of Connecticut before being drafted into the United States Army where he served from 1965-1967. Jerry trained with the 196th Light Infantry Brigade in basic training, Advanced Infantry Training, & Advanced Unit Training for ten months at Fort Devens, MA, Camp Drum, NY, & Camp Edwards on Cape Cod. He was awarded two letters of commendation for his proficiency & the right to be deployed with the advanced party of his unit to war zone "C" in Vietnam. Jerry achieved the rank of Specialist 4th Class & was presented with the Combat Infantryman's Badge. His division received a Unit Citation for their service in Vietnam.

Upon his return to the United States, Jerry graduated from the Programming and Systems Institute in 1968 & was employed for five years with Pratt & Whitney's engineering department. He then went on to have a very successful 45 year career as proprietor of the No leak Roofing Co.

Beyond his honorable military career and impressive professional career, Jerry is committed to veterans' affairs & to community service. He has been Commander & Chaplain of Veterans of the Vietnam War. He has been Senior Vice Commander & Chaplain of Catholic War Veterans Post 1166. He has been Chaplain of VFW Post 1840. He has been Chaplain of the American Legion Post #75. He is presently Commander & Chaplain of DAV Chapter #7. Jerry is an honorary member of the Middlesex County Historical Society for over 30 years. He is a charter member of the Russell Library Veterans Writing Group. Jerry is also a board member of the Greater Middletown Military Museum. Jerry, a member of Elk's #771, helped found the Elk's Veterans Kayaking Program which is dedicated to providing a better life style for disabled veterans & their families.

In addition to his service to country & community Jerry is also an accomplished athlete. He was inducted into the Middletown Sports Hall of Fame class of 1994. He competed in the "Empire State Building Run Up" for 8 years & won the 50 & over division in 2001. Jerry won a bronze medal last year at the Boston University World Indoor Rowing Championships & went on to establish a new American & World Record for the 70 & over division completing 6000 meters on a rowing machine. In September of this year Jerry was the eldest of participants to complete the "22 K" or 14 mile forced march for the prevention of suicides among our veterans.

For these reasons & many more, the Middlesex County Chamber of Commerce is proud to present the 2020 William J. Pomfret Veteran community Service Award to Gerald E. "Jerry" Augustine.

Past Recipients of the William J. Pomfret Veteran Community Service Award:

2003-C.J. Larry Marino, 2004-Robert Wamester, 2005-Jack Monahan, 2006-Philip Cacciola, 2007-Arthur Lerner, 2008-Richard Anderson, 2009-Ronald Organek, 2010-John Krasnitski, 2011-Peter Galgano, 2012-William Currlin, 2013- Jeremiah T. "Jerry" LaMark, 2014-Norman Hanenbaum, 2015- Michael Rogalsky, 2016- Lawrence "Larry" Riley, 2017-Thomas Goglia, 2018-Morton "Morty" Pear, 2019- Reginald "Reg" Farrington

ACCEPTANCE SPEECH

Because the 2020-2021 Covid-19 pandemic was ongoing, the ceremony had to be virtual and was shared online. This is a copy of my acceptance speech.

In the first week of October 2020, I decided to visit Fort Devens in Ayer, Massachusetts, 120 miles northeast of my home in Middletown, Connecticut. Exactly fifty-five years ago in October 1965, I arrived there to begin basic training with the Army's newly reactivated 196th Light Infantry Brigade, 3rd battalion/21st Infantry. I was attending UCONN previously and didn't question my draft notice as I felt it was my duty to serve.

While looking over the now vacant three-story brick billets, the adjacent parade field, and the surrounding landscapes that was our home for ten months while training, many memories came over me. I thought about how close we had become. We truly were brothers. In July of 1966, our brigade of 4,000 were deployed to war zone "C" in Vietnam to build the Tay Ninh base camp near the Cambodian border and Ho Chi Minh trail. Our mission was to protect Saigon, the capitol of South Vietnam, from the infiltration from the North Vietnam Army and the Viet Cong. We did this through search & destroy missions, ambush patrols, and helicopter assaults.

What I've learned through my military career is that there is a strong bond of camaraderie that develops like no other, and it lasts throughout one's lifetime. This is why I feel now that it is important to me to reach out and serve my community and fellow veterans.

I am truly honored to be this year's recipient of the William J. Pomfret community service award. I would like to thank the past honorees for choosing me. You have honestly touched my heart.

I would like to close with one thought. Please keep your thoughts and prayers with those men and women who are presently serving in the military keeping our freedoms protected. God bless them all.

Gerald Augustine

ELK'S VETERAN OF THE YEAR

In January of 2021, I was notified that I had been chosen the Elk's Veteran of the Year of B.P.O.E. Elk's #771. It was an honor that they recognized me for the hard work helping to establish the Veteran's kayaking program and building and maintaining the kayak racks and storage areas, and becoming veteran of the year in our community.

Dear Lord:

We honor our veterans who gave their best when called upon to serve and protect our country. We pray that you would bless them for their unselfish service to preserve our freedoms, our safety, and our country's heritage. Please bless them for the hardships they faced, for the sacrifices they made, and for their many different contributions to America's victories over tyranny and oppression. Amen.

Gerald Augustine

Acknowledgements

I would like to thank the following. If it wasn't for them, my story certainly wouldn't have been told.

1ˢᵗ Sargent George Irizarry, A Vietnam combat veteran who joined our round-table group at the Hartford, Connecticut Vet Center. We became very close to the point that we now call ourselves "brothers." He has been pressuring me for over five years to write "my book" and called it "a permanent legacy that you will leave behind for future generations of veterans that will read about a remarkable veteran that never quit and accomplished many things permanent. You are doing the right thing my brother." I owe so much to George.

Hartford Vet Center, When I joined the weekly round-table group at the vet center, I didn't realize there were veterans out there that had similar issues to what I had been going through since we were discharged from the service. As time went on, we became so close knit that we found a therapy amongst one another that truly helped with our coping of our everyday struggles.

Liz Petry & Christy Billings, For eight years now, I have been a member of the Veterans Writing Group at the Russell Library of Middletown, Connecticut. These ladies have volunteered their time and effort to establish and manage a diversified veterans writing group. The premise has been to tell our personal accounting of what our specialty was while serving in the military and how that duty fostered.

Larry Riley, A very much respected public figure in our community. Larry, also a Vietnam veteran, was serving as commander of "Veterans of the Vietnam War," a local fellowship, when I first joined them in 2010. I considered Larry as my mentor as he guided me through the trials and tribulations of this new endeavor in my life of joining these veterans military organizations.

Past recipients of the William J. Pomfret Veteran Community Service Award, I am honored to have been chosen to receive this prestigious award by this group and to be recognized as being a colleague of them.

Gerry Wright and Raymond H. Gustafson, I share with them the atrocity of being affected by the spraying of herbicides, not only on us, but the effect it carried onto our heirs. I thank Ray for including me in his 2020 published book, *Agent Orange: An Insidious Legacy.*

Betty Pear, My companion, supporter, and registered nurse who most graciously watches over my well-being, whether it be during the writing of this memoir, taking my seven daily medications, or seeing that I keep important appointments. She has been a Godsend to me that she tolerates my disabilities of being Bi-Polar and having many PTSD issues.

Tom Goglia, An Air Force, Vietnam Veteran, and bronze star recipient. I thank Tom from the bottom of my heart for believing in me.

GOD

In Retrospect

I now think back to my experiences with the Vietnam war. I believe every citizen should know what it was like to serve in that unpopular war. No matter what their duty was, the serviceman's stories must be told. Everyone who served has a different story and everyone was affected in one way or another.

When I returned home, I was extremely restless and became a work-a-holic. Anxieties set in, and by the early 1980's, I was appointed into a two-year day treatment program at the Newington, Connecicut veteran's hospital. I therefore performed my work at my self-employment business on weekends. I have been married three times, nearly four, and found that no one could live with me. I worked alone as hardly anyone could work with me because of my behaviors. I went through helpers like there was no tomorrow. My mission was to complete set goals in my way only.

I have had recurring boils and skin lesions. I have had my fifth lumbar disc removed at the VA hospital due to blunt trauma during my tour of duty. I still have chronic pain from that injury. I have had jungle rot on my left hand. I have had a period of seizures. I have had five episodes of kidney stones. I have had recurring nightmares of returning to Vietnam combat.

I have malignant melanoma and have had twenty-eight lymph-nodes removed from my axilla. No one told us about the effects of the spraying of the herbicides. I recently had a tumor removed from my neck. I presently am being treated for high cholesterol, high blood pressure, urology problems, and PTSD. I have arthritis. I lost a high percentage of my hearing and have been provided hearing aids by the veterans administration. My disabilities include being bi-polar.

My combat experience had a lasting effect on my family. My eldest son has Asperger's disease, as well as arthritis and many health problems. He played with my combat gear that I sent home unwashed. The herbicides most definitely affected him. His disabilities never allowed him to work. He is my 100 percent dependent. My middle son committed suicide at age thirty-eight and was diagnosed having PTSD. He was a college graduate with honors and has never had a meaningful job. My youngest son has schizophrenia, also a college graduate, and never worked due to his disabilities. He is now suicidal. He lives with my third ex-wife. He stays in his bedroom most of the day and doesn't leave the house. He has been committed to a hospital numerous times.

I will never become a grandparent (life's pursuit of happiness). Serving in Vietnam certainly had a detrimental result of my well-being.

NOT ALL WOUNDS ARE VISIBLE!

Glossary

AIT	Advanced infantry training
AO	Area of operation
APC	Armored personnel carrier
AUT	Advanced unit training
CIB	Combat infantryman's badge
C-4	Plastic explosive putty
Charlie	Viet Cong or North Vietnam regulars
Claymore	Self detonating, concave shaped, above-ground mine
Deros	Date expected return from over seas
F-4	Phantom jets; carry rockets and/or bombs
Friendly Fire	Rounds accidentally fired upon our own troops by our own military
Gook	derogatory term for Asian derived from Korean war
Grunt	Infantryman, usually non-commissioned
Ho-Chi-Minh Trail	underdeveloped road from North running through South Vietnam, Laos, and Cambodia
Hooch	Dwelling for civilians
Horn	Military radio with microphone
Hot Zone	landing zone under fire
Huey	nickname for uh-1 helicopter
Jody	The "friend" you left behind-he dates your girlfriend or wife
Klick	1000 meters or .62 miles
Lifer	career military person
LP	Listening post
LZ	Landing zone
Medivac	Evacuation to hospital by helicopter

Mortar	Muzzle loading light ground cannon
M-14	7.62mm rifle used in training and partial Nam use
M-16	The standard Vietnam combat rifle
M-60	Standard machine gun of Vietnam, slang - "pig"
NVA	North Vietnam Army
OCS	Officer candidate school
Platoon	usually ¼ section of company- Approx. 25-40 soldiers
Point	First soldier in patrol
P-38	C-ration folding can opener supplied in case
REMF's	Rear echelon M-F's, all soldiers not on the front lines
RPG	Rocket propelled grenade
R & R	rest and recreation-3 to 7 days
Slick	UH-1 helicopter
Spider hole	Enemy fox-hole, usually camouflaged
Squad	10 or less men, 4 squads in platoon
Strac	A soldier of outstanding qualities
Viet Cong	National Liberation Front, fighting S. Vietnam Govt.